Hone

FROM THE BESTSELLING TEAM THAT
BROUGHT YOU *DETONATE* AND *PROVOKE*

Hone

How Purposeful Leaders Defy Drift

GEOFF TUFF
STEVEN GOLDBACH

ILLUSTRATIONS BY TOM FISHBURNE

WILEY

Copyright © 2026 by John Wiley & Sons, Inc. All rights reserved, including rights for text and data mining and training of artificial intelligence technologies or similar technologies.

Published by John Wiley & Sons, Inc., Hoboken, New Jersey.
Published simultaneously in Canada.

No part of this publication may be reproduced, stored in a retrieval system, or transmitted in any form or by any means, electronic, mechanical, photocopying, recording, scanning, or otherwise, except as permitted under Section 107 or 108 of the 1976 United States Copyright Act, without either the prior written permission of the Publisher, or authorization through payment of the appropriate per-copy fee to the Copyright Clearance Center, Inc., 222 Rosewood Drive, Danvers, MA 01923, (978) 750-8400, fax (978) 750-4470, or on the web at www.copyright.com. Requests to the Publisher for permission should be addressed to the Permissions Department, John Wiley & Sons, Inc., 111 River Street, Hoboken, NJ 07030, (201) 748-6011, fax (201) 748-6008, or online at http://www.wiley.com/go/permission.

The manufacturer's authorized representative according to the EU General Product Safety Regulation is Wiley-VCH GmbH, Boschstr. 12, 69469 Weinheim, Germany,
e-mail: Product_Safety@wiley.com.

Trademarks: Wiley and the Wiley logo are trademarks or registered trademarks of John Wiley & Sons, Inc. and/or its affiliates in the United States and other countries and may not be used without written permission. All other trademarks are the property of their respective owners. John Wiley & Sons, Inc. is not associated with any product or vendor mentioned in this book.

Limit of Liability/Disclaimer of Warranty: While the publisher and author have used their best efforts in preparing this book, they make no representations or warranties with respect to the accuracy or completeness of the contents of this book and specifically disclaim any implied warranties of merchantability or fitness for a particular purpose. No warranty may be created or extended by sales representatives or written sales materials. The advice and strategies contained herein may not be suitable for your situation. You should consult with a professional where appropriate. Further, readers should be aware that websites listed in this work may have changed or disappeared between when this work was written and when it is read. Neither the publisher nor authors shall be liable for any loss of profit or any other commercial damages, including but not limited to special, incidental, consequential, or other damages.

For general information on our other products and services or for technical support, please contact our Customer Care Department within the United States at (800) 762-2974, outside the United States at (317) 572-3993 or fax (317) 572-4002.

Wiley also publishes its books in a variety of electronic formats. Some content that appears in print may not be available in electronic formats. For more information about Wiley products, visit our web site at www.wiley.com.

Library of Congress Cataloging-in-Publication Data is Available:

ISBN 9781394304530 (Cloth)
ISBN 9781394304547 (ePub)
ISBN 9781394304561 (ePDF)

© ILLUSTRATIONS BY TOM FISHBURNE | MARKETOONIST.COM
COVER DESIGN: PAUL MCCARTHY

SKY10122836_073125

For everyone we get to interact with – families, friends, clients, colleagues, random people on the street – who have taught us to be believers in the power of human behavior to create change. And especially for Martha, Michelle, and our respective parents and kids, who have most directly helped us to learn to change our own behavior over time.

Contents

PART I WHAT IT MEANS TO HONE 1

Chapter 1 The Chef 3
Chapter 2 The Problem with Drift 19
Chapter 3 The Nervous System of Strategy 29
Chapter 4 The Craftsman 49
Chapter 5 Wiring the Nervous System 61

PART II HONE YOUR ORGANIZATION 77

Chapter 6 Chief System Designer 79
Chapter 7 The Director 91
Chapter 8 Principles of System Design 99
Chapter 9 A Recipe for Change 113
Chapter 10 Walking the Talk 129
Chapter 11 The Rock Band 139

PART III HONE OUR COLLECTIVE CHALLENGES 151

Chapter 12 Widening the Lens 153
Chapter 13 Minimally Viable Thoughts: Honing Our Future 163
Chapter 14 Reflections on a Trilogy 181

Notes 191
Acknowledgments 195
About the Authors 199
Index 201

PART I

WHAT IT MEANS TO HONE

Chapter 1

The Chef

"Honing is simultaneously a maintenance and a meditation."

—*Flannery Klette-Kolton, Chef*

Being a chef in a high-end restaurant is no easy task. Every night, you are expected to conjure up innovative and mouthwatering dishes that not only tantalize the taste buds but also dazzle the eyes and satisfy the soul. Along with being original, you must also be consistent, replicating each culinary masterpiece with unwavering precision, night after night, so that returning guests can relive their extraordinary dining experiences. Your relentless pursuit of perfection unfolds in a crowded, often overheated kitchen, where tempers can easily rise, and serious injury is only one small miscalculation away. Your busiest days are when the rest of the world is unwinding – weekends and holidays. Amid this chaos, you must balance razor-thin margins and the competing demands of staff, investors, customers, and even friends and family. Your artistic vision must shine through, but you must also turn a profit. No wonder there is a high failure rate in the restaurant business.

Working as a private chef cranks up the heat to an entirely new level. We don't mean caterers who manage the logistics of serving hundreds of dishes at weddings or large parties – that's a different kind of "hard." We're talking about private chefs who craft exquisite dinner parties in the intimate settings of people's homes or unique locations. These chefs create personal, interactive culinary experiences in unfamiliar kitchens, under intense scrutiny, and with nowhere to hide. Indeed, working in someone else's kitchen means the customer is literally able to watch every move – an extreme form of operational transparency even in an era of open-kitchen restaurants. Every host has a different vision for the evening, whether it's an important business dinner, a casual gathering of friends, or a holiday meal for extended family. The ambiance can vary greatly, even with repeat clients.

And that's just the atmosphere. Imagine walking into your workplace and having your tools perform unpredictably each time. For a chef, that means dealing with pots and pans of varying quality, ovens and burners that heat differently, and changing humidity levels that affect baking. Plus, there's the challenge of finding plates and silverware in unfamiliar places. And let's not forget the guests who change their dietary preferences at the last minute: "I know I said I eat anything. What I really meant was anything . . . as long as it doesn't have onions."

Flannery Klette-Kolton, one of four artisans we'll spend time with in *Hone*, explained to us the difference between being a chef and being a private chef.

> My menus are all individualized. If I'm cooking a dinner for you, your kitchen and guests and desired experience are way different than my other clients. Like [my client] Carrie – her stove is different.

So is her plateware. So is her palette and that of her guests. So my ingredients need to be different. In a restaurant, the main goal is consistency. Let's say you mosey up to a bar seat and order steak au poivre and it's the best steak you have ever had. It's at a fair price. It's well executed. You love it. The last thing you want is for the restaurant to change it up the next time you come back. So they need to hit that consistency note to please their guests. In my world, nothing is ever the same – the kitchen, the equipment, the guests.. . . I'm constantly making micro-adjustments.

If the job of the chef is a high-wire balancing act, being a private chef is like doing it blindfolded on a different tightrope every night.

A Chef's Devotion

Born in 1984, Flannery Klette-Kolton has lived that world for half her life. A New York City native, she started expressing her love for cooking at an early age, creating "cafés" for her parents when she was eight. They would wait outside – because, of course, the restaurant was full – until Flannery escorted them to a table set with an elaborate meal: Think watermelons carved into baskets (which most people couldn't do at any age, let alone eight). At 12, she would feign illness to come home and watch Food Network, which at the time was focused on educational programming. Flannery's family loved food and cooked a lot, in addition to enjoying New York City's varied restaurants. The same was true for Flannery's best friend, Lauren Gerrie. After they finished college, they decided to cook for a friend's *Great Gatsby*-themed party on a rooftop in Gramercy and received a lot of encouragement from the guests to create something bigger: "This is so great. You should do this." So they did. They launched bigLITTLE GetTogether, a catering company, to build out their dreams.

They hustled. Flannery went to culinary school. Lauren worked in restaurants. They got referrals for catering events, but what the chefs wanted to do was more innovative. They created ticketed dinners where guests would arrive dressed in the style of a certain theme to spectacular meals. An early breakthrough came when, over a meal of shabu-shabu in the East Village, another chef friend introduced them to Gwyneth Paltrow, who decided to feature them in the early days of Goop. They took full advantage of the increased followership and started to focus on special, curated dinner parties, not catering. In the early 2010s, both Flannery and Lauren appeared on – and won – *Chopped* on Food Network. In 2017, Flannery was selected to represent the United States at the Copa Jerez, a unique international cooking competition held in Spain where chefs work with sommeliers to pair courses with sherry. Flannery and her sommelier partner, Kerin Auth, won the most creative pairing award.

When you spend time with Flannery, you can't help recognizing that she is absolutely dedicated to her craft and is energized by two things: a deep empathy for her clientele and a dedication to the process of getting better, one gig at a time. She is programmed to pay attention to the details that will delight her guests.

> You have to pay attention to people's "isms." Their language. Their tone. What do they say their favorite foods are? Do they talk about a special set of plates they never use? What do they show excitement at? They typically forget that two months ago they told me all these things and then it magically reappears in front of them at a party. I'm a people pleaser and I'm trying to pick up on what pleases every one of my clients. A lot of people do this [just] to make money. My [true] payment is seeing someone enjoy what I've created. It's an energy exchange.

When you consistently delight your clients, the money takes care of itself. We asked Flannery if she's ever lost money on a gig. Not once. She also has never had a client stiff her. Even on her worst gig – where there was a protest outside, the pots didn't work on the induction burners, and the rented oven was faulty – Flannery and Lauren managed to "MacGyver" their way through the creative use of seemingly inadequate tools to an amazing service for the 80 people in the next room. They put the guest experience first and adjusted to figure it out. Happy guests equal happy client – and, despite all the complications, they delivered the goods and the client was satisfied.

The fact that the 80 guests at the front of the house had no idea that Flannery was having the worst day of her career in the back of the house tells you all you need to know about Flannery's North Star: to create the best possible guest experience, starting with incredible empathy for what the guests would love. She has recently migrated away from five-course, individually plated menus to more family-style service. Her main gigs now involve cooking on sailboats for the Sailing Collective, a sailing charter company, where some of her minimalism is driven by necessity given the small "galley kitchens" in which she now works. She explained how one of her goals at this stage in her career is to ease the pressure guests feel in a fine-dining setting and to make the food less "precious." We were surprised to hear that explanation and asked her to expand further about the connection between food, pressure, and the overall guest experience.

> I want my food – and my experiences – to be approachable. With family service, you can take more of this dish if you want and less of that. You don't feel obligated to eat what's on your plate.... [It's so different] when you go to someone's mom's house, and they serve you liver and onions and inside you're saying FML and staring at this plate of food in front of you. It's socially awkward for everyone to see you not eating and having other guests wondering, "Why isn't she eating?" I can literally see them having an internal conversation about it. At the end of the day, I don't want guests to feel like they have to perform for me; they don't need to push food around their plate.

Flannery has developed her craft over the years by watching and learning from thousands of individual guests and their reactions to her food, presentation, and presence. Just as she has learned to add the optimal amount of seasoning and flavors, she understands how to ration her own presence. She can intuit when to be "part of the conversation" and when to be part of the background; it's all part of her craft.

HONING, NOT SHARPENING

We both count ourselves as lucky to have personally experienced Flannery's evolution over the years as guests at her dinners. On one occasion, we got into a deep conversation about knives while watching her prep. We were curious why chefs seemed to all have their own knives.

On some reality TV cooking shows, there's even a saying when cooks are fired from a kitchen: "Pack your knives and go."

Flannery explained that chefs take great pride in their knives, often investing in high-quality blades designed to last a lifetime. Knives make food consistent by allowing the chef to create uniform pieces of the food. Knives make food visually appealing by enabling the chef to cut and assemble food into unique, attractive presentations, like eight-year-old Flannery's watermelon baskets. And sharp knives are essential for safe, fast work: They require less pressure to slice through food, reducing the risk of slipping that can occur when a dull blade momentarily sticks into an object. Great chefs see their knives as extensions of their own hands. Curious about the ritual of knife care we both have watched chefs execute before they start work, we asked why chefs need to sharpen their knives before every use.

Flannery quickly corrected us. Chefs aren't sharpening their knives. They are *honing* them. Amateurs use their knives for years without honing; they get dull and then end up in dire need of sharpening and repair. Professionals hone their blades every day to *keep them sharp*. Flannery went on to explain what honing was and why it is different and critical:

> Imagine the edge of your knife being made up of tiny teeth. When you coarsely sharpen your knife, those teeth [become] wider and more separated. And when you more finely sharpen your knife, those teeth become narrower and narrower. Eventually, you get a knife that feels like it has had the most amazing Invisalign and they are perfectly in line with each other. The honing rod isn't actually sharpening your knife. It's like brushing your teeth. It's making sure none of those teeth are snaggling back out, basically keeping them in line. The more you use your knife and the more you cut on rough surfaces, [the more] the teeth start to pop out and move away from each other. Honing effectively buys you time before you need to sharpen your knife again.

This is the work of honing. It doesn't sharpen the knife; it keeps it sharp. Flannery continued to muse about honing, with words that we found inspiring:

Honing your knife is both a maintenance and a meditation. You are taking the minute before you go into your day to ground yourself, taking the minute to recognize with your body, with your tools, that you're about to approach your craft right now. You're taking a minute to put your best foot forward by focusing on what matters most. You're going to put the sharpest edge of your knife forward into your gig.

You actually can sharpen your knife *too* frequently – it leads to negative consequences like thinning the blade, making it weaker and more susceptible to bending or breaking. It also can change the blade's geometry, negatively impacting performance and precision. For us, "honing, not sharpening" is a metaphor for how successful businesses keep their competitive edge. It also led us to realize that business leaders can learn a lot from artisans who pursue excellence in a craft over a lifetime. As such, in addition to Flannery, we'll meet and profile three other artisans throughout this book: Onne van der Wal, a renowned and award-winning nautical photographer; Sam Pollard, an Academy Award–nominated filmmaker; and two members of the rock band Our Lady Peace.

THE SIREN SONG OF TRANSFORMATION

Business leaders could learn a profoundly useful lesson from this practice of chefs and the other artisans we'll meet in this book. Today's leaders seem to be highly focused on increasingly frequent transformations (akin to knife sharpening), when in fact they would be better served by building daily habits to *hone* their organization like a chef hones a knife.

We understand the current inclination to transform. Whether on account of digitalization, the onslaught of artificial intelligence, the looming reality of climate change, the possibility of changing trade patterns, or the demand for radical cost restructuring, leaders everywhere are seeking to overhaul their organizations to become more competitive. To be sure, change is necessary to avoid being relegated to the dustbin of history. But transformation is a risky way to change. It is a costly and time-consuming process that frequently fails. Just as excessive sharpening can make a knife brittle, the more an organization transforms, the greater the risk of "breaking" the organization due to wear and tear.

Most executives overestimate how often businesses need to be transformed. Like sharpening a knife, transformation is sometimes necessary. As a rule, it's best to minimize the number of times you do it. Indeed, research suggests that the vast majority of transformation efforts fail completely or deliver only modest results. And they don't come cheap. About half of respondents in a 2022 Deloitte survey of transformation executives said their organizations invest between 1% and 5% of annual revenue on transformation programs, and roughly another quarter of them indicated an investment of 6% to 10% of annual revenue – and many of them thought they *had still underinvested*.[1]

The lure of transformation is understandable; the payoffs can be huge. In the early 2000s, LEGO® was facing serious financial trouble. They had diversified too much and strayed from their core product (bricks). The company underwent a significant restructuring, refocusing on their core product, streamlining operations, and embracing collaborations like licensed themes. This turnaround happened relatively quickly and involved significant changes to the company's structure and strategy, enabling an enormous wave of growth. Netflix has also transformed its business model several times over its history, most notably in the early years, pivoting from DVD-by-mail to streaming.

But such successful efforts, in a relatively short time frame, are rare exceptions, not the rule. A 2020 analysis by Copperfield Advisory, Insider, and the Revolution Insights Group found that only 22% of companies successfully transformed themselves.[2] Despite their cost, transformations are both expensive and mostly unsuccessful at delivering the desired outcomes. Naturally, a few contrarians like us ask why they are so frequently relied upon when business leaders might instead make more continuous micro-changes consistently over time to keep the organization on track. This process of consistent micro-changes is what we'll refer to as honing.

Every organization hones toward a different outcome – it could be how it delights customers, the product or services it creates, or the benefit it creates for society, among myriad possibilities. We believe every organization has something we'll call an "elemental purpose" for which it is built; we'll explore that more in Chapter 2, but for now, think of it as the organization's "North Star" on its journey. But, over time, execution of that purpose wears and tears just like a knife, and so it, too, needs to be honed.

This book is a call to action for leaders to build the capability and mindset to hone their organizations, minimizing – but not eliminating – the need for transformation. Some might say this is just common sense for running a business. We'd agree. However, it doesn't happen as often as it should. Instead of making a steady stream of micro-adjustments, most leaders make huge, strategic changes in a highly episodic manner. Major strategy choices are revisited every few years or when there is a significant change in senior leadership. Once a strategy is set – typically by senior leaders in partnership with a strategy department – it's passed along to others responsible for execution. The strategy is viewed as complete by the senior leaders, who then move on to other issues.

Meanwhile, the folks focused on implementation are left to interpret the strategy and figure out how to bring it to life for their teams. Often, these people weren't part of the strategy-creation process, leading to a disconnect between the original vision and how it's experienced across the organization. When challenges arise, those responsible for implementation typically don't let senior leadership know; they proceed as best they can. As a result, implementation is only somewhat consistent with the original vision, the original vision is essentially shelved, and finger-pointing ensues when things don't turn out as expected.

That's just what's happening *inside* the organization. While the struggle between strategy and implementation plays out, the external world doesn't stand still. Competitors observe the same trends and make their own moves. Technology advances and evolves, creating new possibilities for delighting customers or reducing costs. Customers' desires shift based on their experiences with other businesses. Before too long, the strategy that was "set" and supposedly good for several years has become obsolete, leaving the company vulnerable to competitors who are more agile and responsive to change. And of course, by that time, with that much drift, there is no choice but to engage in costly and painful transformation exercises.

Even a dull, blunted company doesn't go down without a fight, of course. Various individuals at all levels of the organization recognize the changes in the marketplace and do their best to adjust how they operate in response. They probably don't change their formal "strategy," but they do make changes in how they run the business. They put in place new policies and procedures, they change up their offerings, they change prices . . . in other words, they "run" the business by choosing what to do in the moment. Because strategy is simply the accumulation of choices that any organization makes (more on this later), that essentially means execution is driving strategy – exactly backward from the way it's supposed to be.

All this dysfunction causes substantial *drift*. We'll examine drift in detail in Chapter 2, but for now, think of it as similar to a ship moving toward its destination but slowly moving off course over time. Drift is often imperceptible at first but catastrophic eventually – and it is compounded by the fact that the correct course itself shifts as well because external factors shape it.

To stay sharp and resilient, today's organizational leaders must shift from episodic transformations to continuous honing. That's what this book is about.

The Meal Ahead

Chefs don't just hone their knives, of course. They continuously take stock of their entire operation, taste-testing each batch of food to confirm seasoning levels, meticulously reorganizing their kitchens for maximum efficiency, and watching their guests closely to see what food is returned versus eaten. This is true even in large kitchens with numerous sous-chefs. Shouldn't senior leaders be at least as invested in running their businesses? We think they should. *Hone* is our attempt to explain why and how such hands-on management is becoming ever more critical even at the top of organizations.

The book builds on the thinking we've shared with readers in our previous books, *Detonate* and *Provoke*. It is the culmination of an (unplanned) trilogy about managing in the face of uncertainty. *Detonate* presented the idea that many of the so-called "best practices" businesses adhere to are actually outdated orthodoxies that must be challenged to effectively meet the demands of a rapidly changing marketplace. In that book, we introduced the concept of a "minimally viable move," an approach to managing an organization through smaller, purposeful, and less risky changes. In *Provoke*, we presented the idea that most critical uncertainties eventually resolve, and companies that recognize the shift from "if" something will happen to "when" it will happen can act earlier to gain a competitive advantage. We argued that too many organizations wait too long to act and thus miss the opportunity to shape the future that is best for them. In *Hone*, we examine what should happen once the playbooks have been dismantled and the best future possibilities have been provoked, offering a highly pragmatic approach for leaders to course-correct in small, constant ways to ensure they achieve their objectives.

In the following chapter, we will explore in more detail the concept of *drift:* what it is, why it happens, and why leaders need to care about it as a problem. Chapters 3 and 5 will examine the concept of the *management system*, the oft-forgotten, oft-ignored fifth box of the Strategy Choice Cascade, a tool that many of our readers will know we are adherents of – in part because it originated at our old firm Monitor Group (acquired by Deloitte, where the two of us are principals today). We will argue that as the (often hidden) drivers of how individuals and organizations behave, management systems are the nervous systems of business and leaders need to pay way more attention to them. As a palate cleanser of sorts, in Chapter 4, we'll introduce you to Onne van der Wal, a photographer of stunning artistry who is also a master of the business side of his craft.

In Part II, beginning in Chapter 6, we will share our view that the CEO must be the overseer of all management systems in the organization as chief system designer (a concept we introduced in *Provoke*). In Chapter 7, we'll meet Sam Pollard, a filmmaker whose work as a director demonstrates the ways that leaders outside the boardroom need to design management systems. Chapter 8 will outline some of the key principles of system design, while Chapter 9 will reveal how to apply these principles to problems of increasing complexity. In Chapter 10, we will share a story closer to home by discussing how we leveraged different management systems at Deloitte to hone our own strategy over the last decade. Part II will end with our final profile subject: two members of the rock band Our Lady Peace, whose enduring career in the notoriously fickle music industry is a fascinating case study of how to hone your product while remaining true to your elemental purpose.

In Part III, we will look at system design across multiple organizations. Chapter 12 provides a framework for this type of system design, then, consistent with how we ended our earlier works, we will share "Minimally Viable Thoughts" in Chapter 13 on the application of our framework to a major societal issue – the clean-energy transition. Finally, in Chapter 14, we reflect across all of our writing over the past eight years.

Back to the Kitchen

As we prepare to dive in more detail into how to hone, let's return to the world of Flannery Klette-Kolton. Falling in love with the process of honing is as important (if not more so) as the outcome of any one event (or financial quarter). If you're truly dedicated to improving your craft, or pursuing the elemental purpose of your business, the process of getting better is much more likely to be a successful and enjoyable path than episodic interventions.

> The one thing that hasn't changed is the passion to please my clients. That's always been there. That's my underlying motivation – to be well received – and [to fulfill] the duty of care that the client has placed in me. But even in those situations where the client is happy, after every gig, Lauren and I would always ride home together making notes for next time.

The experiences that Flannery creates for her clients have meaningfully evolved over the years based on what she's seen and learned. Flannery's food in the earlier part of her career was highly influenced by travel, taking bits and pieces from cuisines and different cultures she immersed herself in. Her dishes frequently pull in elements from Southeast Asia, Mexico, or the Mediterranean. She mixes and matches to create new takes on her original creations.

Those original dinner parties were fancy, multicourse dinners where each course was a beautiful, Instagram-worthy plate of food.

Over the years, partially by watching how her guests experience her food and each other, and partially by necessity from cooking at sea, Flannery has further stripped down her style to the bare necessities of creating amazing and delicious food simply, and terrific experiences. This isn't always easy on sailing boats.

> You're moving. I can't reiterate that enough. Burner-wise, it's like a camping stove. The oven is like a toaster. I describe it as 20 little people at an Aerosmith concert with Bic lighters. Two fry pans, three pots if you're lucky, a cutting board, a baking dish, and a few mixing bowls – that's your equipment. Cooking pasta is the most annoying because you have a big pot of boiling water on a moving boat and it's hard to have that and a pan of sauce on at the same time – it doesn't fit. Catamarans are a bit more stable because of the two hulls but monohulls tilt a lot. And people are coming in and out of my space constantly.

So Flannery had to adapt. Much like a poet discovers freedom within the constraints of a sonnet or haiku, Flannery has a newfound sense of liberation in the compact galley of a boat. Her food is increasingly stripped down to what matters: well-seasoned and executed quality ingredients. But attention to detail is still important – she described an example of one of her very simple tomato sauce recipes that she frequently sees people in restaurants get wrong. When using San Marzano canned tomatoes, she instructs people to use the tomatoes *only* and not the sauce they are canned in, which is overly acidic. Yet, to her frustration, some people pour the whole can into the sauce to increase yields, versus removing the tomatoes and squishing them in the pan by hand.

Details still matter in her simple food.

> I no longer sacrifice flavor or ease of eating for the sake of the dish. There's a dish I love to make a few variations of with roasted red peppers, feta, and walnuts. I used to think I needed to transform those ingredients into something unexpected – like a gel or a coulis or a terrine. But now I'm like, f– that, you know what's really cool and delicious? Just those flavors. It doesn't need to be so contrived.

Not only has Flannery's food changed over time as she's seen what matters, but the way she has become part of the experience has also changed. Previously, she might have been stressed by the presence of someone talking to her in the last few minutes before service, lest the precise timeline that had been created be compromised. But now she's relaxed about the preparation process, recognizing that her personality, her demonstration of cooking techniques, and the show of being able to create this deliciousness on a rocky sailboat is part of her guests' experience.

> It's okay if it takes five more minutes for this dish to come out, so that it comes out good. Nobody's in a crazy rush. If a guest is in the kitchen and wants to be talking to me, it's just as important that you take your focus off of cooking for five minutes to have this conversation to give them this sense of experience that they know that you're available to them.

We took away several lessons for business leaders from our conversation with Flannery. First, there is nothing more important than truly empathizing with the guest and what they want their experience to be. Even more importantly, forcing what you think their experience should be on them is potentially a recipe for disaster. Second, always take the time to figure out how you can improve your craft, even by just a little bit; incremental improvements add up over time. And finally, you have to see the process of improvement as your lifelong work; if you don't love it, then you won't do it.

Let's begin.

CHAPTER 2

The Problem with Drift

The capability to combine a learning mindset with hands-on precision is the hallmark of great leaders who have accomplished extraordinary things with their organizations. Looking beyond all the tech founders-turned-billionaires who display these qualities, consider visionaries like Howard Schultz, who turned a local coffee wholesaler with a handful of retail locations into the global coffee juggernaut Starbucks; Sara Blakely, who spent years perfecting the design of Spanx before launching her company; or Henry Ford, who innovated as much around production methods and work schedules as he did around engineering of the automobile. Their ability to dream big while mastering the details has been key to their success.

Yet somewhere along the way we seem to have collectively decided that our most senior leaders should be grand visionaries, not detail people. Their job is to see the opportunity, declare a bold vision, rally the troops, and designate responsibility for execution. They should keep their eyes firmly fixed on the horizon and not dirty themselves with any concerns about the details or mechanics of the ship propelling them forward. They should be confident and inspirational, not dissuaded by day-to-day setbacks. Right? No, not at all.

A leader who focuses only on the big picture won't necessarily lead her organization to catastrophe, at least not right away. But she can set in motion the foundation for a more common and insidious cause of organizational failure: drift.

As readers of our previous books will know, we both enjoy being on boats (although only one of us – Geoff – is obsessed with them). It's easy for a boat to drift off course. Subtle shifts in wind, currents, or sailor error can cause the boat to head in the wrong direction. It's usually not a big deal. If we notice that waves, wind, or tide are impacting our route, we can adjust using the controls of the craft, compensating for unforeseen environmental factors. From the smallest dinghy to the largest cargo vessel, this is the discipline of boating.

But sometimes the "drift" is so slight as to barely be perceived. If it goes on long enough, the boat can end up significantly astray. On larger vessels, this might be noticed by crew members who don't want to bother the captain by calling attention to it. So it persists longer than it should. This is the most dangerous type of drift: small, imperceptible changes in vector that steadily pull the vessel off course over the long haul. When the boat finds itself in uncharted waters, it needs to massively adjust course to return to its original path or even to avoid disaster.

Organizations drift, too. Small deviations from a set strategy may add up over time and then require massive adjustments (transformations) to bring the organization back on track. Just like in boating, the role of the leader in an organization should be to captain the organization through its strategic journey, regardless of whether she's leading a small startup, a large conglomerate, or a governmental agency.

In many ways, it's easier for organizations than for boats to drift off course. Boats have a very clear, usually observable destination they are sailing toward. They often have sophisticated instruments that allow the captain to immediately see their position, direction, and velocity. Organizational drift is harder to notice because the destination is often less precise than a specific set of coordinates. For example, a business might be aiming to be the market leader in its industry. What it means to be the leader and how the markets are defined are not as clear as lines of longitude and latitude. Further, in boating, the vector of travel is easily measured. In businesses and large organizations, the question of whether we may be heading in the right direction is not always clear. Finally, and most confoundingly, in boating, the destination stays static. Drift only happens because the boat's vector changes. In organizational leadership, drift can happen either because the direction of travel changes or because the "right" destination shifts over time.

THE CAUSES OF ORGANIZATIONAL DRIFT

In complex, large-scale organizations, there are myriad possible causes of drift. In fact, we don't think a complete list could ever be compiled. Pretty much anything that impacts the direction of an organization or its destination could be on that list. That said, there are a few causes of drift that we observe most frequently. For ease of organization, we separate those causes into *external* factors and *internal* factors.

External Factors Driving Drift

On the external front, the most frequent causes of drift tend to be actions by competitors, changes in technology, changes in regulations, and evolving customer needs. Actions by competitors are often the most obvious: We see them impacting strategies in nearly every industry, by changing pricing decisions, entering new markets, and acting and reacting to each other. Actions by competitors clearly have the potential to impact both the direction in which a company is heading and their desired destination. Consider the actions by Uber when faced with different entrants. Upon Lyft's original entry on the lower end of the market, Uber added UberX. When Gett entered some of its markets with the ability to reserve cars in advance, Uber added the same capability. In short, when faced with unique competitive threats, Uber added equivalent features to their platforms to protect their market share. Unlike many companies facing similar challenges, though, they broadened – instead of entirely changing – what they offered their customers. Their services still result in users being able to get where they want on-demand without their own vehicles. They combatted drift by staying true to the elemental purpose of their business (more on this later).

Changes in technology have the potential to materially change the potential economic viability of different business models. Technology can quickly make some business models an order of magnitude better or an order of magnitude cheaper, facilitating entry into the market by new competitors. With that comes a constant need to adjust on the part of the organizations already in the industry. Consider the explosion in the wellness industry enabled by the intersection of biometric tracking and advances in understanding human longevity. We now see businesses devoted to providing customers with regular bloodwork, new supplements, exercise routines, and physical examinations. There is an entire ecosystem of podcasters devoted to the topic. This field is clearly going to change the economics of traditional healthcare organizations and the healthcare insurance industry, so leaders of those businesses will need to examine if they have been pushed off course and whether the destination they were heading toward still makes sense.

Government regulations have the potential to materially change the context for virtually all organizations. When new policies are enacted, they change the vector and destination for nearly any business in the impacted market. Indeed, government regulations and laws are among the most powerful forces shaping how organizations function (more on this in Chapter 12).

Finally, changes in customer behavior can shake up a market and lead to meaningful organizational drift. When's the last time you were in a long line and wished there were a simple, technology-driven way to avoid the wait? If you are such a person, you're in good company: Both of us proudly seek out technology to help us skip lines in daily life. Whether it's mobile ordering at coffee shops, expedited processing options at borders, or depositing a check via an app, today's world abounds with options to meet the universal customer desire for increased convenience. Of course, these changes also cause companies to respond haphazardly to updated customer expectations – and risk drifting off course.

The good thing about exogenous causes of drift is that they are pretty easy to see and tend to be easier to rally support to address. More insidious causes of drift happen *inside* the organization – often driven by human tendencies – and sadly tend to go unnoticed for far too long.

Internal Factors Driving Drift

To understand internal forces that push organizations off course, consider the widespread practice of changing people's roles every few years. This happens in many organizations because human beings have strong desires to grow and make their mark. As a result, leaders have a natural inclination when they come into new roles to undertake a partial or complete rewrite of what existed before. If you multiply that by the number of leaders across a large organization, that's a lot of pivoting over time. Without a meaningfully constant long-term direction, it becomes impossible to determine what it means to be on-course. And the more senior the leader who is changing, the more broadly the knock-on effects are felt. We should challenge the orthodoxy that everything needs to change when leadership changes, but it's hard to overcome the personal need for the new leader to show they are having an impact by doing things differently.

A second major internal cause of drift is that many senior leaders focus almost entirely on setting strategy, yet neglect the internal actions needed to ensure that strategy is carried out. Readers of our earlier work will recall the five-box Strategy Choice Cascade from the *Playing to Win* framework, which we introduced in Chapter 1. Many leaders get fixated on the "Where to Play" and "How to Win" boxes and overlook the later parts of the cascade that bring these ideas to life in the real world. In particular, they often ignore the fifth box, which asks, "What management systems are needed?"

Although we will dig deeper into management systems in later chapters, think of them for now as everything that managers use – formally and informally – to motivate behavior: performance reviews, HR processes, budget structures, and more. We see them as among the most powerful levers for organizational change. If leaders ignore them, an organization can drift off course. But when given proper attention, these same systems can help steer things back on track.

Unfortunately, management systems are often brushed aside as routine "execution" tasks for others to handle. Once a strategy is set, leaders may turn their attention elsewhere. A typical pattern emerges: The CEO and other top executives engage in periodic strategy sessions, then schedule only occasional check-ins – quarterly or twice a year – to look at past performance data. This routine can become self-reinforcing because many executives find strategy work more exciting than the day-to-day mechanics of ensuring the organization actually *lives* the strategy. Yet it is precisely this follow-through – testing whether the strategy is delivering results and whether the organization's behavior aligns with it – that prevents drift. Without it, years can pass before anyone notices the need for a painful course correction.

Another reason drift takes hold is a direct consequence of the one above: Because senior leaders pay little attention to management systems, old or ineffective ones never get removed. These systems accumulate like barnacles on a ship's hull, hindering an organization's maneuverability. This buildup isn't solely due to leadership inattention; often, functional teams within the organization change their own systems in response to specific problems or crises without thinking through how these changes affect the rest of the organization (and because there's no senior leadership oversight, no one is able to referee competing initiatives). Even when a system is formally "retired," parts of it can linger for years because people keep using it out of habit or convenience. Over time, the organization ends up weighed down by layers of overlapping rules, processes, and tools.

It is exactly because of this potential for drift that senior leaders need to give management systems the deliberate, ongoing attention they deserve – both to avoid going off course and to help correct the path when inevitable detours arise.

THE POWER OF MANAGEMENT SYSTEMS TO ADDRESS DRIFT

Drift happens. The question is how we can optimally configure organizations to minimize it and/or episodically use it as an advantage. The answer (as discussed): Flip the orthodoxy around the role of the C-suite – especially the CEO – in strategy creation and execution. Stop them from lingering at the top of the cascade and instead give them the ability to tinker directly with management systems. Management systems are inherently things to be fiddled with. CEOs should use them to test hypotheses incrementally, quickly observe the outcome, and then test more ideas. With the most senior leader in the organization literally managing the controls, we can start to think of strategy more as a flow than a stock. With a strong sense of direction and the direct ability to spot and correct against drift, any CEO is bound to be more successful in keeping his or her organization on track (more on the role of the CEO in Chapter 6).

This hands-on approach captures the spirit of "management by walking around" pioneered at Hewlett-Packard and later popularized by Tom Peters. When Bill Hewlett and David Packard regularly walked the factory floors, they weren't merely making symbolic appearances; they were gathering direct, unfiltered feedback about how management systems were functioning in practice. This immersive approach allowed them to spot subtle signs of drift before they became visible in performance metrics, and to make immediate adjustments based on ground-level reality rather than abstract reports. Similarly, CEOs who embrace this philosophy can detect the early symptoms of misalignment between strategic intent and operational reality, making course corrections before drift becomes entrenched.

"ELEMENTAL PURPOSE": ANOTHER TOOL TO ADDRESS DRIFT

As we noted earlier in this chapter, sometimes the "drift" is so slight as to barely be perceptible. If it is perceived, it may be noticed by someone who doesn't have the ability or influence to call attention to it, let alone fix it. In situations like this, the organization continues on without major problems in the immediate term.

You can't know if you're off-track, though, if you don't know what the track is. Much like the planned navigation route of any traveler, every organization needs to have a sense of direction. Sure, a strategy offers a sense of direction, but in stormy weather or in unexpectedly strong currents, you can't wait for a new one to be set; you need to orientate and adjust *now*. An organization's elemental purpose can act as an internal compass for that direction. Many organizations have an *ornamental* purpose – sets of words, way too heavily debated and wordsmithed, that find themselves on posters but rarely infuse their way into decision-making. We're talking about something different. Just as the ancient Polynesian wayfinders relied upon their deep understanding of celestial bodies and ocean currents to spread their civilization across the Pacific, organizations must use their (often innate) elemental purpose as a North Star – a steady point of reference to constantly measure against to keep a true course.

What exactly is an "elemental purpose"? Simply put, it's the reason an organization exists. It's not a mission statement per se, but a higher-order objective that articulates the reason shareholders, employees, and customers are drawn to the organization. In some organizations, the mission statement does come close. Consider Patagonia's mission statement: "We're in business to save our home planet." This, in fact, articulates a strong elemental purpose. If Patagonia's stakeholders – especially employees – are ever in doubt about a decision regarding the company, they can check it against that maxim. On the other hand, Apple's mission statement could be construed to be "to create technology that empowers people and enriches their lives." This may somewhat motivate employees, but it reads to us more as a customer marketing statement. It doesn't capture the essence of why Apple exists. As we think about the essence of Apple, it strikes us that far more important to its purpose are user-centric design, innovation, and quality in everything it does – its products, its retail experience, and even its environmental stewardship. We wonder if its elemental purpose – in line with a quote often attributed to Steve Jobs – might be something about showing consumers a thrilling experience before they can express their need for it.

Think of just about any long-lived company and you can probably come up with a good enough hypothesis as to what their elemental purpose might be. Take Costco as another example. While its big-box stores are known for selling almost everything under the sun (and in bulk quantities to boot), its commitment to value, transparency, and a positive customer experience brings a cohesion to its brand that creates loyal customers. Perhaps "put overt customer value on display in every way, every day" captures it? For the tax preparation company H&R Block, it might be something related to "garnering trust through simplicity."

Elemental purpose is a somewhat enigmatic concept, but it can be helpful to leaders and managers up and down the organization who sense drift. With the accumulation of many layers of management systems, competitors acting aggressively, and technology advancing, knowing the essence of why your organization exists can be an effective North Star to determine if you are on or off course. We'll return to this concept periodically throughout the book.

But first, let us return to the concept of "management systems" – the intricate web of formal and informal systems that shape how people think and act inside an organization. In the coming chapters, we will explore management systems in greater detail, thereby laying the bedrock upon which the rest of the book is built. Understanding how to hone management systems is the crucial skill that determines whether a leader will chart their company to sustained success or watch it drift into irrelevance. To begin, however, we must first lay a long-running business shibboleth to rest.

Chapter 3

The Nervous System of Strategy

"Culture eats strategy for breakfast."

As strategists, the two of us would be long retired – Geoff sailing every day and Steve doing whatever crazy fitness program he's into – if we had a dollar for every time someone threw this quote in our face, usually as an edgy challenge to the need to do the strategy work that we consider important. We have a lot of admiration for management theorist Peter Drucker, to whom that quote is widely attributed. Interestingly, there is no evidence he actually ever uttered this phrase. In fact, the Drucker Institute (and they would know, right?) said that Drucker never said it. He writes in his 1992 book *Managing for the Future*, "Culture, no matter how defined, is singularly persistent." The quote is consistent with Drucker's body of work, which often emphasized the human side of management. The idea that a firm's culture can override the best-laid plans is also Drucker-esque.

But we think the quote is highly problematic, and frankly outright wrong, because it presents culture as somehow separate from strategy. The quote makes it sound like culture is some amorphous smoke monster (with apologies to those of you who never watched the TV show *Lost*) that can't be controlled or managed. That's simply not the case. Culture doesn't just magically materialize due to the charming, charismatic, quirky, or laissez-faire nature of senior executives. Culture is a strategy choice. As a leader, you have the power and choice to change culture to fit an objective – or to recognize that an objective is a bridge too far. Separating the two concepts is just lazy thinking that Drucker wouldn't approve of.

Since we are contradicting a pervasive business orthodoxy, we think it's important to expand on why we see culture as interwoven with – and derivative from – strategy choices. We'll revert to the Strategy Choice Cascade as our preferred framework for describing an organization's strategy. In short, the cascade articulates that strategy is defined by making five *interconnected* choices:

1. *What is your winning aspiration?* This is the overarching goal that the organization is trying to achieve.
2. *Where will you play?* This is the way the company defines the markets in which it competes.
3. *How will you win?* This is how the organization can advantageously differentiate itself from competition in those markets.
4. *What capabilities will you need?* These are the capabilities needed to deliver against the first three choices.
5. *What management systems will you need?* This answers the question of how a company will motivate its people to deliver against the first four choices.

Roger Martin, who developed the cascade framework with colleagues at Monitor Group, has often said that the heart of strategy is set by the first two choices: "Where to Play" and "How to Win." We agree. But that does not mean that strategy ends there. Over the years, based on countless client engagements, we have come to believe that the most common cause of failure for business strategy occurs when executives don't give enough attention to the "bottom" of the choice cascade. If the "Where to Play" and "How to Win" choices are the heart of strategy, the "Necessary Capabilities" and "Enabling Management Systems" choices are its nervous system. To us, this is an important metaphor. In biology, the nervous system is essentially the body's command center. For humans, that means a complex network of nerves and cells that carry messages between the brain, spinal cord, and the rest of your body. The nervous system enables all five senses by processing inputs and sending them to the brain. It sends signals from the brain, via the spinal cord, to muscles, causing them to contract. It regulates involuntary bodily functions like breathing and heart rate, and it plays a crucial role in higher-order cognition. Put simply, the nervous system allows you to perceive the world around you, react to it, and control your body's functions. That's what capabilities and management systems do for organizations.

The Importance of the Bottom of the Cascade

Building capabilities is like practicing a new movement such as riding a bike. Learning to do it correctly and making the movement second-nature requires an investment of time and practice. Think of management systems as regulators of dopamine for behavior – good and bad – inside an organization. Dopamine is a crucial part of the body's nervous system. It is a neurotransmitter associated with reward, motivation, and learning. It's largely responsible for the feeling of euphoria and joy when you first sustain momentum on a bike and don't topple over. It thus plays a crucial role in reinforcement, goal-directed behavior, and habit formation. It works when something that the body determines is pleasurable (though not necessarily "good") – receiving praise, achieving a goal, eating a sweet – triggers a chemical release, causing a feeling of well-being and satisfaction. The brain links the actions that led to this pleasure with dopamine, so it creates the desire to repeat the actions that led to the release. Actions lead to rewards, which lead to the desire to repeat the action until this association becomes automatic and a habit is formed.

Broadly, management systems define "what good looks like" – and set limits and guardrails inside an organization. They determine everything from how performance is evaluated to how sales and other financial targets are set to who gets highlighted at the company off-site. Management systems motivate the collective behavior and habits of the human beings inside any organization. And do you know what they call the collection of behavioral habits inside a company? Culture.

Yes, culture, which we'll define as the *collective behavioral tendencies of the organization*, is a powerful force. People tend to want to behave in a manner consistent with norms, save for a minority who explicitly enjoy being "countercultural." But culture doesn't magically appear based on company posters and slogans. It is created and hardened over time by the choices leaders make through management systems – the oft-overlooked fifth box of the choice cascade. When you change a critical management system, you can very quickly change behavior and culture.

A Powerful, Potentially Virtuous Cycle of Reward

Why do management systems promote specific behaviors so well? Human beings tend to have a common desire for growth, improvement, and achievement. The dopamine pathway described above provides a biological underpinning. But evidence in the fields of evolution and psychology also helps explain why. From an evolutionary standpoint, the drive to improve and acquire resources has been crucial for survival. Those who strive to better their circumstances have historically had a higher chance of survival and reproduction, so it could be ingrained in our human makeup. From the field of psychology, Maslow's hierarchy of needs has self-actualization at the top of the pyramid. In our opinion, this is synonymous with realizing one's full potential – in other words, succeeding. Neither of us could point to a single client or colleague who didn't want to succeed.

In *Detonate*, we discussed the concept of "Me, Inc." – the notion that not everyone inside an organization is looking to maximize shareholder value; they are looking to maximize the value of their own accomplishments and benefits. The way they define that value varies. Some look to monetary rewards. Some to promotion and climbing the ladder. Some to a consistent work–life balance. Whatever the value, common across all workers is a desire to do a good job at what they're asked to do.

Since management systems broadly define what good looks like inside an organization, they have the potential to create a powerful virtuous cycle. Humans have a desire to succeed, and management systems point them toward a goal. If they have the capability to achieve that goal, they get a dopamine reward for having achieved it, ingraining the behavior. But humans can get frustrated too when success isn't easy – or the definition of success is changed, making it harder to achieve. That's part of the reason why transformation is so hard on people – it involves substantial behavior changes very quickly. Humans are motivated best by achievable goals and demotivated by those perceived as unachievable. The work of psychologist Edwin Locke in the field of goal-setting theory proved across numerous studies that specific, challenging goals that are in reach result in more effort than goals perceived to be out of reach.

THE DANGER ZONE: SETTING AND FORGETTING MANAGEMENT SYSTEMS

There are plenty of cautionary tales of companies that forget to tend to management systems at their peril. Let's take, for example, the story of Nokia, once the leader of the mobile phone revolution. From one vantage point, they can be seen as a company that succumbed to its own success and the management systems that got it there. In the late 1990s, the company was on a tear, with revenue growth between 1996 and 2000 multiplying by five times along with a 150% increase in headcount. That they were able to achieve this while they faced supply chain challenges is testament to management systems they installed to drive efficiency and deliver short-term performance.[1]

As devotees to the idea of a balanced innovation portfolio (see *Detonate*), we might immediately wonder whether Nokia had forgotten to innovate in adjacent and transformational spaces as they ran the core for maximum production. But they hadn't. They were fully aware of the need to stand up future sources of revenue and even took steps to set up a New Venture Board and the Nokia Ventures Organization. Both proved prescient in identifying "early signal" trends such as the Internet of Things, spinning up new ventures and rolling them into the core business to access funding and scaled attention. The problem? They forgot to hone by evolving the core management systems that rewarded behavior consistent with efficiency and scaled production. As a consequence, the new ventures organization had insufficient management attention and funding, and did not produce innovations consistent with their recognition of the trends. Though there were many contributing factors (most associated with management systems that could not support rapid growth and diversification), ultimately Nokia failed because it never found the elusive "third leg" of growth it was seeking when Apple, Google, and Samsung showed up to the mobile phone scene. It did see this need coming, but it failed to change its core constructs to create the behaviors that might have led to more success. Indeed, if you comb through any company's garden of management systems, typically you'd find a lot of weeds.

A Taxonomy for Management Systems

We intentionally take a broad definition of management systems when we perform strategy work. As stated above, they can be anything that shapes and motivates the behavior of the people inside an organization. We define them broadly to ensure we capture the many informal management systems that shape behavior (e.g., imagine a day when a CEO surprised everyone by starting to dress casually . . . how long would it take for other employees to dress similarly?). But there are a few relatively common categories of management systems that we see across most organizations.

Let's examine each in turn.

Formal Management Systems

Formal management systems tend to be the ones that are easiest to spot in part because they're typically well-documented and out in the open. They might be written in the playbooks of the organization or communicated to employees and other stakeholders through company webcasts or team meetings. In theory, they should be connected to and supportive of "upstream" (in the cascade) strategy choices, but they often are not. There are five that we think are most powerful:

1. Performance evaluation
2. Budgets
3. Organizational design
4. Metric design
5. Public commitments

Performance Evaluation

Performance evaluation is probably the most powerful formal management system because it *literally* defines what good looks like at an individual level. People like being recognized for their work and these systems play a crucial role in providing that validation. Indeed, people want to be told how they can be successful, and performance evaluation systems give them that framework and provide feedback at the same time.

When Monitor was acquired by Deloitte, we witnessed firsthand the impact of subtle changes in performance management systems. Most professional service firms – especially private partnerships – measure the performance of their most senior people using metrics related to revenue and profit delivered to the firm due to their efforts. Monitor had a performance evaluation system where its partners could share revenue (i.e., "credit") generated with other partners in an unlimited way. This was designed to encourage teaming and leverage diverse expertise for clients. However, it led to many partners receiving strong performance reviews despite the firm not being as profitable as it needed to be. Why? Because the target for revenue per partner was set too low for a management system that enabled unlimited sharing. Consequently, Monitor had a reputation for excellent client service but being a little less operationally buttoned-up.

Deloitte, on the other hand, encouraged teaming by enabling the sharing of "sales" successes (reflecting who was influential in the sale) among partners but "managed revenue" (reflecting what partner is responsible for delivering the project) could only be claimed by one partner. By having two separate goals, Deloitte successfully encouraged both teaming *and* financial accountability. We saw a distinct change in the behavior of Monitor partners in the periods pre- and post-acquisition by Deloitte. Prior, there would be many partners on a single engagement, probably more than necessary (which sometimes overwhelmed our clients and teams). After, the partners tended to be more thoughtful about when and where we showed up for the greatest impact.

Performance evaluation is a very powerful behavioral tool. But be cautious – the sheer power of this incentive can be hard to control, leading to unintended consequences. For example, if people are told that maximizing sales is the key to being highly rated, don't be surprised when they figure out how to "game" the management system to boost sales or push uncomfortably hard to close deals when the quarter is ending, even if these moves may not be the best thing for a long-term customer relationship. Similarly, if customer service representatives are rated solely on their Net Promoter Score survey responses, they may start encouraging customers to "rate me 5/5 please," which can undermine the effectiveness of the rating system, as well as turn off customers. In 2016, there was a widely reported challenge at a large company where sales incentives, coupled with a high-pressure culture, resulted in significant unethical behavior. This led to the resignation of the CEO and other executives. (In Chapter 5, we'll explore incentives in more detail when we examine the role of binary versus continuous targets.)

Budgets

After performance evaluation systems, the budgeting process is probably the next most obvious and influential formal management system. Most managers of businesses or functions spend a substantial portion of their time fighting for budget, protecting their budget, justifying their budget, or looking for more budget. How often have you heard a leader say, "This is important . . . but we don't have the budget for it"? Well, if it were important, the organization would *find* the budget for it. It follows that a senior leader seeking to influence managers' behavior would leverage the budget or budgeting process as a powerful tool for motivating what their people do. For instance, if an executive wants to encourage a manager to prioritize profit margin maximization, they could implement a policy whereby future budgets are directly linked to the magnitude of cost savings realized in the current period.

To understand how powerful such formal management systems can be, consider two fictitious companies: Acme Inc., which uses traditional incremental budgeting, and Zephyr Corp., which has adopted zero-based budgeting. At Acme, managers often engage in "use it or lose it" spending at the end of the fiscal year to ensure their budgets aren't reduced in the next period. This leads to wasteful expenditures and a lack of cost-consciousness, but it also maintains morale and perhaps even fosters innovation and experimentation, as managers may use the excess funds to pilot new projects or test creative ideas that they might not have been able to pursue under stricter budget constraints.

In contrast, Zephyr's managers must justify every expense from scratch each year, forcing them to critically evaluate the necessity and value of each line item. This approach encourages cost-saving and a continuous focus on efficiency. However, it also requires more time and effort from managers during the budgeting process and can lead to chronic stress from fear of starvation. Ultimately, the choice between incremental and zero-based budgeting depends on the organization's priorities and desired behaviors. Incremental budgeting may be suitable for stable, predictable environments, while zero-based budgeting can be a powerful tool for organizations seeking to drive cost-consciousness and adaptability in dynamic, competitive landscapes.

When combined, performance evaluation systems and budgets can dramatically shape behavior, positively or negatively. Although being well-funded is frequently interpreted to show where leadership priorities lie, securing funding is just a critical *first* step in launching new initiatives; financial resources alone don't ensure success. Without corresponding recognition in performance evaluation metrics, even well-funded projects can falter as employees naturally prioritize activities that directly affect their assessments and rewards. When Steve was at Forbes 25 years ago, there used to be two magazine offshoots called *FYI* and *ASAP*. They had decent editorial budgets, but ad sales only took off when the sales team was specifically measured on pages sold in those issues.

On the flipside, it can be equally demotivating to assess people against something for which budget is not provided. It's akin to providing them with an unachievable goal and has the potential to make people give up because the goal is unattainable. Providing budget and setting performance targets can be a powerful combination, but only if they work in unison.

```
                    MANAGEMENT SYSTEMS
            FORMAL                      INFORMAL
1. Performance Evaluation    1. Unwritten Rules
2. Budgets                   2. Decision Rights
3. Organizational Design     3. Executive Questions and
4. Metric Design                Behavior
5. Public Commitments        4. Meeting Norms
                             5. Orthodoxy
```

Organizational Design

Organizational design often works in concert with budgets and performance evaluation because it defines where and how money is allocated and who conducts the performance evaluation. Many organizations are matrixed in some way between business line and geography, and the vector with the "power of the pen" in evaluations and budgets tends to dominate. Drawing these lines and boxes also creates frequent management system dilemmas – for instance, how to allocate and share resources across structural lines because of the human desire to "get credit" for one's work. For example, if the best-suited employee to serve a customer sits outside the responsible group, two supervisors must agree to create an exception, complicating performance evaluation and reward systems. The more exceptions required, the less effective the management system becomes.

Metric Design

Underpinning formal management systems, you will almost always find highly observable metrics: key performance indicators (KPIs) and/or objectives and key results (OKRs). Effectively designed dashboards that track and report KPIs can further fine-tune or nudge behavior by focusing attention on a specific set of data. KPIs and OKRs are frequently used in concert with performance evaluation, but not always. For instance, measuring only topline sales is likely to incent growth with less profit discipline, while focusing solely on the bottom line might lead to greater cost discipline at the expense of market share. Neither is necessarily "correct." The most effective metrics can be dynamically adjusted to reflect what matters most in near-real-time, ensuring alignment with the organization's current priorities.

Public Commitments

Public commitments or communicated information, such as financial estimates made by the CEO or CFO to the analyst community, are another form of formal management system. Public commitments are among the most powerful determinants of their own focus and, by extension, that of their organization. This type of system is hard to "fine-tune" because commitments are difficult to alter once they have been announced, particularly if the board holds the CEO accountable to this goal via another important management system – her pay package.

Similarly, commitments to operate within a legal or regulatory framework, along with any subsequent disclosures about the quality and execution of those commitments, carry significant weight and influence behavior throughout the organization. Take sustainability, for example. Though commitment types vary in different regions of the world, we're living through a unique period where sustainability commitments, which have been quite common in the world of financial performance, are now being translated into nonfinancial disclosures. Being new to the practice, many organizations have set very aggressive sustainability targets, some without a plan or sufficient infrastructure to bring those targets to fruition. As more companies around the world are required to disclose their performance against these targets because of regulations, we are seeing organizations take target setting more seriously, often resetting targets and developing formal plans for how they will hit them. Given our penchant for learning and optimism, we do wish that resetting goals wasn't always viewed as "backsliding" since companies need to be given the grace to learn and tune commitments in ways that make them more tangible, immediate, and actionable. Indeed, being accused of backsliding is a barrier to creating necessary feedback loops about what it will take to make the world more sustainable!

All of these formal management systems examples are from the world of traditional businesses. But a very important example of formal management systems is government laws and regulations. Indeed, these are the "apex predator" of management systems as they shape behavior for all organizations and humans within their jurisdictions. Laws and regulations may not be within the sphere of influence of business decision-makers, but they are absolutely tools for governmental leaders as they set their strategies for what they want to achieve.

INFORMAL MANAGEMENT SYSTEMS

Unwritten Rules

The other category of management systems is informal. These are cues within an organization to behave in a particular way. Often informal management systems are directly associated with formal systems. For instance, the timing of formal processes like strategic planning, financial reporting, and customer engagement may have some formality to it. But there are often unwritten rules for how these things are done. There is unlikely to be a written rule that strategic plans must be long and boring PowerPoints that start with reams of data about the market that everyone already knows, but they mostly are! A terrific demonstration of informal management systems came in the movie *A Few Good Men* (1992) when Tom Cruise's character, Lieutenant Daniel Kaffee, is cross-examining Noah Wyle's character, Corporal Jeffrey Barnes.

During the direct examination, Barnes is asked to show in the Marine guidebook where it explains what a "code red" is (the offense for which the defendant is on trial). Barnes cannot show it in the guidebook because such an entry does not exist. During the cross-examination, Kaffee asks Barnes to show him in the guidebook where the mess hall is. Barnes answers, confused, that this information is not in the guidebook, either. Kaffee then says sarcastically, "Do you mean to tell me than in all your time at Gitmo, you've never had a meal?" Barnes says, "No, sir. Three squares a day, sir." Kaffee asks, again sarcastically, how he could possibly know where the mess hall is if it's not in the guidebook. Barnes answers, "Well, I guess I just followed the crowd at chow time, sir." That is literally the definition of an informal management system – following the crowd at chow time!

[Cartoon by Tom Fishburne: a man stands between a small sign labeled "RULES" with three items listed, and a much larger blank sign labeled "UNWRITTEN RULES".]

Decision Rights

Who gets to make what decision – including who is asked for their opinion (otherwise known as "decision rights") – is a critical informal management system. Sometimes they are formally documented but are more often tacitly understood. Decision rights are critical because they guide several important factors in how choices are made – who frames the choice, what perspectives are included, and how fast the choice is made. Someone who can frame the choice can subtly do it in a way that benefits "Me, Inc." Change the decision-makers, change the decision. Decision rights are often fuzzy, leading to all kinds of efforts to influence important choices.

Executive Questions and Behavior

One of the most powerful (and often overlooked) informal management systems lies in the questions posed by senior executives. How often have you left a meeting with next steps driven primarily by the questions the senior person asked? "Our CEO asked whether we had considered expanding our target market to include segment Y; let's go run down that analysis before we go much further." The more senior the person, the more likely their questions are interpreted as mandatory work – which quickly turns to mayhem if different members of the team have different interpretations of the question. As the two of us have experienced as we've assumed more senior roles in organizations, we often hear through the grapevine things that we've supposedly asked people to do based on something we said that had very little to do with our actual intention. Many leaders may not realize that their words carry so much weight that the words (or even body language and tone) are themselves an informal management system.

 We frequently tell the story of an executive we know who wanted to push his organization to innovate in ways that didn't involve touching the product: Product feature changes in his industry tended to be a very expensive way to innovate and were easily copied. However, it became clear to us as we sat through meetings with the executive and his team why the design team kept reverting to fiddling with the product: The executive was downright giddy when the team showed him cool new product features. It was – naturally – perceived that the way to please this executive was through product enhancements. We took the executive aside and told him to stop complimenting the product features and to ask more questions about what they were doing to innovate outside the product. Sounds simple, but this small change had a powerful and almost immediate impact.

Meeting Norms

In addition to questions, general meeting practices can play a key role in reinforcing important behavioral norms. Oura, a company that produces a smart ring that collects data about personal health, opens every large group meeting with letters and stories they receive from customers about the role the ring plays in their life. On a recent *Fortune Next* podcast (for transparency, Deloitte is the sponsor of the podcast), Oura CEO Tom Hale told stories about a customer who had been trying to get pregnant and was using the Oura to track her menstrual cycle. She took a screenshot of the day the Oura knew she was pregnant before she did. Similarly, an NBA player shared a story that his 92 readiness score gave him the confidence to go out and perform well in a Game 6 playoff game. Hale notes that this informal meeting practice plays a key role in keeping the team focused on their elemental purpose.

Orthodoxy

Informal management systems are often created out of reactions to formal management systems. Often ethereal, these derivative management systems are perceived norms and expectations based on company lore, stories, or orthodoxy – a topic we covered in great detail in *Detonate*. Consider one organization we work with, which has a very balanced performance evaluation system. It rates its senior leaders on a mix of qualitative and quantitative objectives across multiple metrics. Even so, there is a cultural perception that the "only thing that matters to getting ahead" is hitting your sales targets. The formal management system is nearly powerless against this perception, so much so that leaders have had to go out of their way to emphasize the qualitative portions of the evaluation system. Indeed, deeply held beliefs often need open public renunciation by a senior leader to counteract. In this company's case, that could include not promoting or even firing someone known to be a great salesperson but not good at working with others. Such an extreme act would send a strong signal that the organization takes things besides revenue generation seriously.

Why Management Systems Matter

When you combine these management systems, you get very strong behavioral signals inside an organization. These signals can powerfully reinforce the strategy of the organization or conversely hinder its realization. In other words, you can have a really great idea for how to create value for your customers, but if you don't motivate your people to behave consistently and in line with your "Where to Play" and "How to Win" choices, that idea will never come to fruition. And more often than not this disconnect is why an organization drifts. Organizations don't get the behavior change needed to move in the right direction.

Here's just one example: We worked with a toy company that believed its most important differentiator was the quality of its brands. The company was structured with "global brand teams" responsible for creating products and marketing campaigns for the brands, and "market organizations" tasked with dealing with customers in the major geographic regions the company operated (e.g., the United States, Europe, Asia). The market organizations sold all the brands to local retail customers and were evaluated on the total company profit in their region. Importantly, the market organizations decided how much money to spend on each brand in its market based on what they expected to be "hot" that year.

Over time, this model presented challenges. Some of its core brands were underinvested in and over time their performance flagged. The company's differentiation hinged on its iconic brands, yet inconsistent and unpredictable annual marketing efforts hindered brand momentum, especially during years in which there was no hot new product for the brand. The management system aligned better with a strategy focused on a diverse toy portfolio rather than individual brand strength. Textbook drift. Eventually, the company changed this system to provide greater control over marketing spend to the global brand teams.

The mistake the toy company made was succumbing to the orthodoxy that simple and clear budgets and decision rights are better at creating outcomes than management systems that lean into the nuance of collaboration. One organization that found a clever way to tackle the interconnectedness of silos within the company was Gillette under the leadership of Jim Kilts, prior to its acquisition by Procter & Gamble. At the time, Gillette had four major brands – Gillette Blades and Razors, Duracell, Braun, and Oral-B – and operated in several regions, including North America; Europe, the Middle East, and Africa; the Asia Pacific; and South America. Like the toy company, Gillette faced the challenge of creating long-lasting brand loyalty from consumers while maximizing sales and profit across all regions and with major customers. Kilts addressed this by designing an evaluation system that forced strong collaboration and shared objectives across the brand and regional teams. For example, the Blades and Razors CEO was responsible for the global performance of Blades and Razors across all regions but could not be highly rated just by hitting the overall sales or profit target. Instead, they had to hit that target in all regions, with their rating declining if many regions' targets were missed. Similarly, regional leaders couldn't achieve their highest performance rating by overperforming on a single brand. They had to hit targets for each brand in their region. Creating this co-mingled performance expectation created strong collaboration on shared objectives.

How Leaders Should Hone Management Systems

Adjusting management systems is the route to avoiding and counteracting drift. Making adjustments is akin to steering the boat. Leaders need to be at the helm of the organization, watching carefully how adjustments are made. Leaders must have strong knowledge of all the management systems within the organization and the ones that truly matter. That's how they can carefully hone adjustments to management systems that change the behavior that will counteract drift.

The payoff can be enormous. Amazon is an overused example of management philosophy – perhaps because the moves that Jeff Bezos made look so clean in retrospect. So, with apologies for returning to that well and for smoothing out the complexities along the way, let's look at Amazon and the collection of management systems that have contributed to its success. Bezos has made it quite clear that he set out to create "Earth's most customer-centric company," arguably Amazon's elemental purpose from day one. The company consistently experimented over time to understand what delighted customers most, and as they learned, they upped the size of the investment in those areas. Their experimentation also produced entirely new businesses – Amazon Web Services, Prime Video, and others. Their data-driven focus makes experimentation on a small scale easy, and they do it consistently.

The bottom line is this: Management systems, formal and informal, work in concert to change behavior. Make the wrong adjustment and you can end up creating confusion or the wrong behavior. Use the right management systems and your strategy will be realized – and possibly create enormous value if it's a good strategy, like Bezos's move into cloud storage. Formal management systems are a good place to start honing – making small adjustments and watching for results – but the executive doing the honing needs to have a hypothesis about what the knock-on implications of their changes will be. Make a change. Observe the behavior. Make another small change and see how it goes. That's leadership.

A New Understanding of Culture

We hope you leave this chapter with a new appreciation for the importance of the management system in the leadership toolkit. As the nervous system of an organization, it provides the levers for motivating and directing human behavior. It critically defines so-called "culture" and whether or not a company can achieve its objectives. Sadly, too many executives generically ask employees to "execute better" without giving guidance for how to do so or providing motivation for what specifically they should execute better. Management systems can help them do that.

Indeed, we will examine shortly how CEOs, in particular, must have oversight over – and the capability to instrument – their organization's management systems. We will explain in greater detail the variations of management systems available to a CEO – and the risks and benefits of different approaches to designing these management systems.

But before we dive into that, we understand that we've asked the reader to digest a lot of dense material in this chapter. So, taking inspiration from chef Flannery's well-paced meals, we decided the next course on the menu should provide an opportunity to cleanse the palate with a profile of an artisan. We'll venture out into the ocean to meet a consummate craftsman and understand how honing has been the key to his enduring success as an artist, entrepreneur, and human being.

Chapter 4

The Craftsman

The sea has been Onne van der Wal's home for as long as he can remember. And like the sea, Onne is constantly restless. Born in the Netherlands and raised in a small fishing village just outside Cape Town, South Africa, Onne has made his own career as a photographer, sailor, ship-repairer, and inveterate tinkerer. Whether it's fixing high-performance racing yachts, meticulously devising his plan for making his next picture, or overhauling his own boats, he's constantly fine-tuning.

In fact, his career and professional life have taken on some of the qualities of the ocean – immense, impressive, but also impossible to pin down. You're as likely to find him precariously steadying his camera on a sleek racing yacht battered by roaring winds as you are to find him sprawled in the belly of one of his own sailboats, using his deep knowledge of shipbuilding to lovingly restore an ailing 50-year-old craft.

We know Onne mainly as an award-winning photographer and a longtime Canon Explorer of Light. He has traveled the world shooting (primarily) the world of sailing by boat, by helicopter, half-submerged in water, and sometimes clinging to a rail with one hand and clicking away with the other. He has published a number of books; his wife, Tenley, runs a successful retail gallery selling his work; and he has been the subject of multiple documentary films.

Consider one of his photographs: *Salmon Fishing in Kamchatka*. It is a study of perspective, how an artist can render depth and spatial relationships on a flat surface. In the foreground, a fish has its head turned sideways with one eye on the viewer even as it seems poised to strike the submerged red fly floating just above its partially open mouth. In the background, a fuzzed-out angler finishes his cast with his arm raised, poised to set the hook. You can just make out a blurry rod, which helps you imagine the line that runs between the two creatures in that exciting, primal, seemingly umbilical way fisherman and prey are connected. Accentuating the distinct yet permeable barrier between the two is a wavy ribbon of water that cuts the photograph almost precisely in half.

The more we pondered this photograph, the more we came to see that wavy ribbon as essential to the photograph's mastery. Here is an artist at absolute ease with – and even seemingly in command over – the mysterious, protean nature of water. He can catch the submerged fish below the surface and the elevated rod and fisherman above in the same image.

Most of Onne's photographs are of sailing, not sportfishing. But we contend that this masterful photograph would not have been possible if Onne hadn't spent a lifetime on or near the ocean.

Salmon Fishing in Kamchatka and the rest of Onne van der Wal's oeuvre make clear that he is near-unmatched in his craft. That alone made him a fascinating subject as we considered how organizational leaders can learn from artisans. But the films about Onne are what really captured our attention. They are (surprise!) difficult to pin down and define precisely. They're kind of about photography but they're much more about life's ups and downs, love and adventure, and messing around with boats. They show the true side of Onne as a craftsman. As we got to know Onne better, it became clear that his seemingly innate capability comes from a lifetime of learning and experiences.

A Machinist's Precision

Though Onne was born in the Netherlands, he did most of his growing up in Hout Bay, a coastal town just outside of Cape Town. As a kid, he kicked around the docks among trawlers and sailboats, gradually getting exposure to an environment centered on the sea. He got to know the fishermen who welcomed the mop-haired kid and (quite literally) showed him the ropes. As he got a bit older, he was given the opportunity to head out on the boats to lend a hand in whatever way he could. He figured out how to make himself useful and, eventually, indispensable.

Conventional schooling doesn't feature heavily in Onne's life story. He admits that he wasn't great at academics. One gets the sense that he could take or leave the type of school where many of us honed our own professional skills. But he does light up when he talks about his time as a machinist apprentice, a four-year training where he was one of a few young White students in a shop full of Black men, an oddity in then-apartheid South Africa. Admittedly, when we sat down with Onne, we knew little about what it meant to be a machinist, or "fitter and turner" as it's known in other parts of the world. But he quickly helped us understand: The shop where he worked made the tooling that enabled large, high-volume machines to manufacture everything from toothpaste tubes to soda-can ring pulls to bullet shells. The work demanded precision – the shop used milling machines, lathes, and surface grinders capable of working to a precision of 1/4000th of an inch (about the thickness of a hair).

Onne's apprenticeship in the shop is partly a tale of a young man learning to work with metal and be precise, envisioning exactly what needs to get done ahead of time, and measuring many times before cutting once. But mainly it's a story of being human – learning from others and helping others. It was in this seemingly dull, mechanistic environment that Onne says he discovered that "buried in me was the capacity to learn and be good with my hands and help other people." The foreman and head instructor of the apprentice school shop played a seminal role in his development. "He was the kind of guy that would *show* you: what this thing is in your hand, how you need to hold it to approach the machine, where you need to cut it, what movement might cause a problem with the machine. He was so amazing about the technique and making sure that this cutter is going in a certain direction, and so on. I learned . . . how to get it right."

Though he loved his time as an apprentice, he was eager to get out into the world. Since he was an adolescent, Onne had been heading out on boats, looking for ways to be useful. An invitation to sail on a family friend's racing yacht introduced Onne to the world of competitive sailing – the family friend was impressed by Onne's breadth of interest and capability and encouraged him to pursue the sport. Onne's talent and dedication soon earned him a position as a watch captain and starting helmsman in his first major ocean race: a 3,200-mile transatlantic journey from Cape Town to Uruguay. To take on this role, he had to complete his apprenticeship at the machine shop in just three years instead of the usual four – a challenge he readily accepted and conquered. Fortuitously his father gave him a "little point-and-shoot camera" to take along for the ride to capture a record of his experiences. So Onne started taking pictures.

As the 1970s gave way to the 1980s, Onne found himself captivated by the allure of open ocean racing. The renowned Whitbread Around the World Race, now known as the Ocean Race, particularly captured his imagination. Through his own resourcefulness, Onne managed to contact and persuade Conny van Rietschoten, a retired Dutch industrialist who had become a celebrated yacht racing skipper, to take him on board the *Flyer II* for the 1981–1982 race. He was kind of a do-it-all on the boat. Technically his responsibilities were engineer, bowman, and general crew for sail trim and helming. But the way he made his impact was to put his machinist skills to work and to constantly hone the workings of the boat – and fix parts that failed – to keep it up to optimal performance.

He also served as the official onboard photographer and movie-camera operator. Based on the experiences he had on his various trans-atlantic crossings, Onne had been approached by American *SAIL* magazine to document the race. Many others might have been intimidated by the assignment; Onne convinced himself that the same steps to planning and executing a precise machine cut could be used to make an extraordinary picture. He spent time experimenting with angles and lighting and camera settings, guided primarily by an ongoing process of learning what pleased him and what did not – an experience that set the foundation for his future life.

Of all Onne's stories from the race, the one about the boom breaking stands out as our favorite. For non-sailors, the boom is the horizontal pole at the foot – or bottom edge – of the main sail that attaches to the mast. On a 76-foot racing yacht, this is a vital and substantially sized piece of equipment. In the second leg of the Whitbread between Cape Town and Auckland, *Flyer II*'s boom snapped in the middle of the night, a potentially race-altering disaster. Thankfully, the ship's engineer had come prepared. Onne explains: "It had broken once before [on a previous voyage], and it's a major slowdown. So before we left, we went to the shipyard's metal shop and said we needed two formed sleeves about five feet long [to serve as possible repair sleeves] and shaped to the boom's profile with holes predrilled to fit." He did the drilling and countersinking ahead of time and grabbed extra screws, drills, and taps to enable the sleeve to attach to the boom, just in case. This was a habit of his: to wander around a machine shop and the boatyard in advance of a race and scavenge random bits of metal and fasteners to add to his stash on the boat. "You can't anticipate things on the boat; they just happen," he told us. Thanks to his general preparation, he fixed the boom in no time.

The *Flyer II* won the 32,000-mile race in a record-breaking 124 days, got a mention in the *Guiness Book of World Records* for their circumnavigating record, and established Onne as a renowned racer, sailor, and photographer.

Onne does not consider himself a tinkerer. He made it abundantly clear in our discussions that he doesn't love the term, even though he is in our minds the ultimate manifestation of someone who will fiddle with something and tweak it until it is just perfect. "To me," he says, "it comes across as a little bit of an amateur guy; if someone is tinkering, most of the time it breaks and doesn't work. I would rather say I'm a craftsman and technical guy."

Regardless of the moniker, it is Onne's attention to detail, sense for "what good looks like," willingness to apply some elbow grease, get his hands dirty, and keep at it until he feels the job is done that we think all business executives can learn from. He is not a perfectionist in the sense that he's comfortable with imperfection, as long as he's able to keep iterating. The result, however, is often near-perfection. For instance, the camera housing device that Onne used to capture the half-submerged salmon fishing image was designed and built by him, exactly fit for purpose. It was not overdesigned nor expensive, but it filled a specific need for his groundbreaking photography business.

An Uncharted Journey

After the Whitbread race, Onne's reputation grew quickly. In 1985, he decided to relocate to Newport, Rhode Island, one of the top sailing capitals of the world. He had visited Newport a few times over the years and was drawn back by the easy access to all things nautical, along with the steady stream of sailing and photography opportunities that came his way there. In 1987, a fellow sailor named Jim Adams, also a harbor pilot and the Photo One chase boat driver, remarked that if he tackled marine photography in a serious and professional manner he could own the market in five years. So he decided to pivot toward full-time professional photography and established Onne van der Wal Photography. His retail operations and multiple spin-off businesses did not yet exist, so he had to survive on commissioned shoots. In practice, he was inventing an entire subindustry as he went along.

Professional photography had of course existed for decades before that time, but very few had tried to adapt the mountain of photo gear for use in a marine environment. A tripod doesn't do so well on a rolling boat. Expensive cameras with corrodible parts don't love salt water. Perfect stillness to accommodate long-exposure shots rarely exists when the wind is howling and boats are responding accordingly. So Onne built his own kit. "When I need something like a fluid gyro camera mount or I need something that maybe doesn't exist, or is very expensive, it is a lot easier for me to just make it. I can follow the train of thought behind the original design and adapt it to what I need . . . I just have to focus on it."

The camera housing was just one of these adapted solutions. As we learned from Onne, one of his favorite things to do is to go to the annual photography expo at the Javits Center in New York City and just wander. He might have a certain shot in mind or a vague notion for a technique he is trying to master, but mainly he just wants to see what is out there. Sometimes he can stop at a display and just stare and think, wandering off in his own mental world (and perhaps to the increasing alarm of the exhibitor and passersby) as he considers how he might be able to use or adapt a piece of technology to his practice. "So many times, my new ideas for photography started at the show and something I wanted to do [but] I didn't know how to get the camera or the technique, [so I] started picking these guys' brains. I would chat to the people that go and display their gear, and I got on board with Canon, Fuji, various tripod and light manufacturers, et cetera. I'm always looking to improve and be one step ahead of the other shooters in my field.. . . It was always 'How am I going to do that?'"

Onne liked the idea of being able to capture images from a partially submerged vantage point, either swimming among the boats with the camera or mounting a camera on a pole from a chase boat. By this point he had met and married Tenley and he used to take submerged pictures of her diving off boats into the water, but he didn't love the fact that, outside of the human subject, you would be left with just the underside of the boat in the shot and nothing about what was happening above the surface. He knew he didn't need to go much deeper than one or two feet for what he had in mind, so the solutions that were out there were generally overdesigned. "I found an Austrian company aimed at the diving industry that could go to 100 feet," but it was too much design and too much cost. The idea, though, inspired him, so he started thinking and tinkering (with apologies to Onne for using his disliked word, for expediency).

> I modified a piece of gear that I found and set out to experiment. For example, I would go [on assignment] to Grenada for the Grenada Sailing Festival sponsored by American Airlines, and I would have breaks of 45 minutes or an hour to work with the idea and show it to others.... Not only do you have to get [the camera] waterproof but the settings of the camera, the focus, the shutter speed, and so on need to be accessible. At the same time, the cameras were getting better and better and going to higher ISOs for the technical parameters and everything.

Though he had a working prototype at all points along the way, it took him about five years to perfect it . . . and we guess he'll continue to adjust as new technology lands on the scene, staying true to his model of continuous improvement and adapting to new technologies.

He has always brought the same persistence and vision to the creation of his images, especially the innovative ones. "I know ahead of time exactly what I want to accomplish, and I keep at it until I get it," even if that means sometimes creating waves with his clients. He told us one story about a shoot he was doing for the marketing department of Hinckley Yachts, a high-end boat manufacturer. "I was shooting in Newport for their Talaria model boat. It has a cockpit and a house with a beautiful shape. What I wanted to do was to stand on the swim platform looking forward and with a 14mm, catch the outline of the house and the lights, and some movement." He suggested shooting the idea but the marketing person said they were out of time.

> We went back to the dock, dropped her off along with her assistant, and I asked the skipper if he would take the boat out for me just before sunset to anchor in front of the Newport bridge. There was a little color left in the sky and the lights of the cockpit and cabin showed up beautifully. I knew that if I left the shutter open, I could get what I was looking for. Your eye doesn't see it because it doesn't have the shutter speed. Like a designer, I could visualize the end product. If I exposed for the interior lights and the last bit

of color in the sky still showing up, I knew I could get the desired effect and nail the shot. I did a long exposure of three to five seconds and shot it and I got it. It's a huge sense of accomplishment [when] they ask, "How did you do it?" It's beautiful, I love it.

That shot became one of Hinckley's go-to print ads.

SAILING ON

We can't come close to doing justice to Onne's extraordinary journey in the space we have here but also can't leave the reader hanging. So far, it's a journey with a happy ending. Tenley and Onne opened their photography gallery in 2001 and it continues to thrive today; go visit it on Bannister's Wharf in Newport if you have the chance. They have three grown children, and their tight, happy family spends a lot of time on the water. Onne's books are distributed around the globe. His first, *Wind and Water*, was published by Little Brown in 2004. *Sailing*, published by Rizzoli in 2013, a book of nearly 200 color photographs and five gatefolds of panoramic images showcasing work from around the world, was followed by *Sailing America*, also by Rizzoli, in 2019. He self-published *Nautical Newport*, in 2013, featuring curated images exclusive to Newport. And right around the time *Hone* comes out, we expect to see another coffee table book called *Jamestown, Rhode Island*, comprised of images from the island that he lives on.

Though it took him a while to realize it, Onne has also become a businessman, in partnership with Tenley. Currently, that business comprises custom photo assignments for boat builders, retail sales, stock photography (a bank of previously shot images to pull from for specific advertising or editorial requests), international expeditions, photography workshops, and lectures. Like any good business, the aspects of what exactly that entails have shifted over time as he has honed his model, building new aspects when new opportunities arise, and shedding others that no longer fit the purpose. Given his attention to the detail of his craft and industry, we are not at all surprised that he added video at just the right time. Together, the van der Wals have had no qualms taking on new and difficult challenges and saying no to projects that are not financially viable or don't align with their values. Onne has always simultaneously had his finger on the pulse of the industry and his hands deep into the operations and management systems of his business.

We mentioned earlier in this portrait that the documentaries about Onne are what made us sure we wanted to profile him in *Hone*. The focus of the first two films is on Onne as boat craftsman as he retrofits two boats. His work on *Snoek*, a 1972 Pearson 36 sailboat, is the subject of *Second Wind: The Tale of a Sailor,* released by PBS in 2019. That was followed two years later, via a partnership with *Soundings* magazine, by a series of videos put out on YouTube and various social media platforms documenting a similarly deep overhaul of *Snow Goose*, a 1986 Grand Banks 32 trawler. Both stories feature the work of a man who methodically tears down an old, tired boat, and rebuilds it by hand. He does it slowly and surely, job by job, setting a vision for even the smallest task, thinking it through carefully and then executing with confidence. He works with wood, paint, fiberglass, electronics, fabrics, and everything in between; it seems as if there is nothing he can't tackle if he puts his mind to it, regardless of whether he has faced a similar job before. We see setbacks, frustrations, small victories, and continual perseverance – sometimes in the subzero temperatures of winter – through to the point that each boat is launched in the warmth of early summer.

Unknown Destination: A Love Story is the latest documentary about Onne, released in early 2025. It is a much different film than originally planned. It was meant to be a story about Onne and Tenley wandering on *Snow Goose* down the Intracoastal Waterway toward the Bahamas. They were to have no strict itinerary or schedule; they would just meander from anchorage to anchorage, to marinas and town docks, exploring local communities as they learned to step away from the demands of business. Instead, it became a love story about a woman in remission from breast cancer on the trip of lifetime with her famous photographer husband – who himself is diagnosed with an aggressive and often fatal form of cancer halfway through the trip. It became the story of Onne as he faced the hardest fix-it job of his life and how he learned to lean on others and mix modern technology with human strength to find, and then travel, his own path to remission.

As we reflect on Onne's polymath career, we realize that while he may be best known for his photography, it is his ability to keep things in focus – to be true to his elemental purpose, close to the sea – that is the real secret behind his multi-decade success.

We asked Onne what he has learned – as a machinist, as a boat engineer, as a photographer, as a father and husband, as a cancer survivor, and as a successful businessman – and how it might be relevant to our readers. He summed it up simply and elegantly: "Determination, persistence, striving for perfection . . . I've spent 80% of my time taking old things and making them better, whether fixing something broken or just continually improving. The rest of it was adapting the new stuff to achieve my specific goal. Of my years being hands-on, I've seen it's not the fastest on the road [who win] but the steady ones. A lot of the time we weren't the fastest . . . but we were the ones who fixed it and kept going."

Chapter 5

Wiring the Nervous System

Steve has been waiting to write this chapter for about a decade. He's been accused (perhaps by Geoff, definitely by others) of being mildly obsessed with the design of management systems and beams with pride in meetings when other Deloitte executives mention them by name. It's impossible to know exactly where the obsession started, but it might have been sparked by an experience his wife, Michelle, had at the DMV over 25 years ago.

Here's the story. Michelle walked into the local DMV, passport and Canadian driver's license in hand, ready to make a simple exchange. She had just moved with Steve to the United States from Canada and needed to swap her Canadian driver's license for an American one. We aren't sure if it is still this simple, but at the time you only needed to prove you were the person in the driver's license and you could make the swap. Straightforward enough, right?

But as she handed over her documents, the agent behind the counter frowned. "This passport," he said, tapping the booklet, "it's fraudulent." Michelle was taken aback. How could her passport, the one she had used to enter and exit the country numerous times, suddenly be deemed fake?

The issue the agent cited was on Michelle's work visa, stapled inside the passport. When Michelle filled in the visa on entry, she accidentally put her first name in the last name section and last name in the first name section. A simple mistake, so she put a line through it and placed the proper names above in the white space. Michelle tried to explain that it was obvious that it was a simple correction, and the correction had been sufficient to get her into the United States in the first place.

But the agent was unmoved. Rules are rules, and if the visa inside the passport didn't meet the strict criteria, it couldn't be accepted by the DMV. The agent asked if Michelle had other forms of ID, as it was necessary to have a certain number of "points" of ID to qualify for the license swap. Passports were enough with the driver's license to qualify. Without the passport, multiple other, less valuable forms of ID were needed.

Desperate, Michelle pulled out her birth certificate. Again, no luck. The form had changed since she was born, and her 1973 document didn't match the current template held by the DMV agent. He said he couldn't authenticate it. Another "fraudulent" mark against her.

In a last-ditch effort, Michelle emptied her wallet onto the counter, showing an expired Queen's University student card, a Canadian Tire rewards card, and her Air Canada Aeroplan membership card, among others. Together, she and the agent painstakingly tallied up the "points" each item was worth (if any) in a bid to reach the magic number that the DMV had determined she needed. There might have even been a high five between the two of them when the total was reached. Luckily, she was able to find enough points among the relics of her Canadian identity to allow her to exchange her license.

As an epilogue, when Michelle opened the ID upon arrival in the mail, she noticed that her license incorrectly noted her as a male, instead of a female. Not surprisingly, she decided that she could live with that rather than risk another trip to the DMV.

Contrast Michelle's Kafkaesque tale with Geoff's recent experience at the border of Azerbaijan. He was traveling to Baku for a climate conference. He fancies himself a pretty organized guy (a polite way of putting it), so he had a printout of his visa paperwork all ready when he approached the Azerbaijani border guard. To his dismay, the guard informed him that despite his careful preparation, he had accidentally applied for his visa for the wrong dates.

Thankfully, Geoff was able to rectify the situation on the spot. The catch? He would have to endure a precisely timed purgatory in the immigration area, waiting for exactly three hours – no more, no less – on a hard, uncomfortable chair before his emergency visa would be granted.

These two stories might seem like mere anecdotes of comical customer experiences, but they reveal something profound about the power of management systems to shape human behavior. In the DMV case, the rigid rules and point-based verification system created a culture of inflexibility, transforming the agent into an automaton that prioritized protocol over common sense. Though the DMV's systems were ostensibly designed to ensure the authenticity of an applicant's identity, Michelle had managed to secure a new license despite presenting an array of expired and easily forgeable documents (and after the two most official documents had been deemed fraudulent!); further, she left the DMV feeling embarrassed and stressed.

In Azerbaijan, the carefully calibrated three-hour wait struck a balance between deterrence and expediency, encouraging compliance while still allowing for human error. Three hours on a hard chair, after all, is probably *just* long enough to discourage visitors from intentionally showing up at the border without a visa – but not so unpleasant as to needlessly punish someone who has made an honest mistake or impede their business in the country. Geoff's experience in Azerbaijan, while undoubtedly inconvenient, was handled with such professional aplomb that it made him appreciate the eloquence of the management system design.

Management System Design

Management systems are the levers of change inside an organization. If used effectively and continuously honed, they can keep an organization on course, negating the effects of drift. This alleviates the need for drastic change via a transformation effort (or, as we can now call it, the attempted overhaul of many, many management systems at the same time with the hope that the design works seamlessly).

Improper management system design typically leads organizations to unsatisfactory results – and, unfortunately, this is common, because it's hard to get design right. Leaders need to design systems that fit the uniqueness of their organizational tendencies (in addition to creating systems that work for the different types of individuals inside their organization). Human motivation isn't ubiquitous, and the "Me, Inc." algorithm will be different for different groups. Plus, there is an unlimited set of plausible management system options that an organization can use. Given this variability, in this chapter we will provide a set of observations and considerations about management system design that a good leader can use in their consideration for how to hone. We will cover, specifically:

- The importance of consistency and congruence
- Binary versus continuous metrics
- Qualitative versus quantitative metrics
- Carrots versus sticks
- Reliable and accurate feedback loops
- "Uninstalling" management systems

While there may never be an exhaustive list of management system design considerations, these six should get the aspiring honer off to a good start.

Consistency and Congruence

Let's return to the example in Chapter 3 of the executive who was giddy about product feature innovation and needed to change the culture of the organization to pursue non-product innovation more frequently. The fact that he had reinforced over the years the importance of product innovation meant that his behavior around non-product innovation needed to be stronger and more consistent. One slipup where he reverted to acting excited about product innovation would undo the hard work he had put in to change perception.

This isn't news to those of you from the world of marketing. Reach and frequency is a critical marketing equation. Consistency and congruence of management systems are effectively the "frequency" of that equation. The more engrained the habit you want to change, the more important it is that there is a consistent and persistent counter-message to create a new habit in its place. Sometimes we encounter leaders who act surprised when the organization does not immediately pivot after a single message to change. We can't underscore enough that it takes hard and constant work to unseat orthodoxies. Back when A.G. Lafley took over Procter & Gamble in 2000 and wanted to refocus the company on consumers, he famously started every brand review asking about the target consumer. Presidents quickly got the message after a number of these in a row – *the question is going to come every time. Be prepared.*

One of our favorite nonbusiness examples is the use of the checklist before and during surgery, pioneered by the surgeon and writer Atul Gawande (and detailed in his book *The Checklist Manifesto*). Seeking to counteract the errors due to lapses in memory or attention that he calls "errors of ineptitude" that strike frequently in an increasingly complex world, Gawande promotes the use of checklists in the operating room to ensure that important steps are not overlooked. The checklist – in the operating room, or in the cockpit, where Gawande drew inspiration from – is a great tool to encourage behavior that promotes safety, or whatever objective you're pursuing.

While consistency in applying a management system is important, it's just as critical that its underlying message aligns with the other systems people experience. Consider the example from Chapter 3 where staff at one company had a pervasive belief that sales were all that mattered in getting ahead, despite the performance evaluation system having a broad array of qualitative and quantitative metrics beyond sales. This could exist because people hear "stories" of how all employees promoted in a given year exceeded their sales targets by 50%. The stories may not be factual – but if they are perceived as true they remain relevant. To counteract this folklore, the company might consider some form of data transparency about the characteristics of who was promoted and their relative performance on sales and other metrics. And it might take more than one performance cycle for the organization to really get the message.

BINARY VERSUS CONTINUOUS METRICS

One key management system design choice relates to the nature of metrics used to drive behavior. An all-or-nothing approach is a binary incentive system. Think of a financial bonus that is paid out in full if you hit a certain sales target: Reach $1 million in sales and get a $1,000 bonus, for example. As we shared in Chapter 3, financial incentives for performance are particularly powerful but can have unintended consequences that don't benefit the customer or the business, such as encouraging the cutting of corners to make numbers.

Let's be clear, though: Binary management systems aren't inherently bad. They have the benefit of being direct and actionable. They can drive behavior that, if targeted at correct levels, can promote win-win behavior. Consider the case of an NFL player coming back from a severe injury. Putting a meaningful, binary "games played" bonus in his contract is a great motivator for the player to focus on doing all the necessary things to stay healthy (e.g., sleeping right, doing rehab, etc.). It's not perfect because factors beyond the behavior can impact the goal, but it can be used properly as a motivator.

A continuous incentive management system is the opposite. A sales commission is a good example – getting 5% for every sale an agent makes is a linear, continuous incentive. The salesperson can have high or low sales, but they always get 5%. This creates a smoother, more gradual incentive structure that encourages consistent effort and discourages the kind of "cliff-edge" behavior associated with binary systems. The challenge that continuous incentives face relative to binary incentive systems is that it's harder to promote "breakout" performance when every incremental success is rewarded equally. Of course, you could combine the two systems by saying a bonus kicks in only at a certain level of sales and escalates linearly from there. It all depends on what behavior the organization is looking to drive.

A continuous performance system that we like is simple stock ownership by employees (not stock option grants, which have binary aspects such as strike prices and performance cliffs). Stock ownership means that as the company becomes more valued by the capital markets, employees also do better. In many ways, this is the beauty of the start-up; everyone is motivated in the same way to get the company to its "monetization event."

One recent example of the possible pitfalls of a binary management system was in the age requirements associated with the

COVID-19 vaccine rollout. It might seem strange to think of a public health campaign as a management system, but governments also have management systems that they apply to their own populations. Indeed, laws and regulations are the most powerful management systems available to policy makers. We also recognize there are varying views on the COVID vaccine, both within the US and around the world. We'd like to put those concerns aside to focus on the design of vaccine management systems purely as an example of the puts and takes of management system design, not as a statement about health policy.

When it came time to administer the COVID vaccine, governments and health organizations established rigid eligibility criteria based on age and location in an attempt to prioritize those most at risk while also administering as many inoculations as possible. For instance, vaccines were available initially for those who were older than 65 years or had severe comorbidities like diabetes. However, binary management systems invite odd behavior when there isn't flexibility in the application. One of us has a friend, Joan, whose daughter was just six months shy of the vaccination age requirement of being five years old. Her daughter also had some meaningful health concerns that made Joan particularly worried about the potential impacts of COVID. Driven by this fear and a deep desire to protect her child, Joan seriously contemplated lying about her daughter's age to secure a vaccine. Joan felt trapped between the rigidity of the system and the very real concern of her daughter contracting COVID and facing potentially serious complications. This situation, while anecdotal, highlights a fundamental flaw in the system: The rules did not align with the nuanced realities of the virus and its impact.

Yes, vaccines are formulated differently for different age groups, but does a difference of a few months in age truly capture all the considerations regarding whether someone should be administered the vaccine, considering underlying health conditions are also a factor? Likely not. The binary system, with its hard-line requirement, failed to account for the gray areas and individual circumstances that influence risk. Accordingly, parents like Joan, acting in what they perceive as their children's best interests, are forced to consider circumventing the system. The ultimate behavioral objective was to achieve widespread adherence to health authority recommendations and vaccinate as quickly as possible. Building some flexibility into a binary management system (for example, in this case, allowing doctors discretion to administer the vaccine if the individual was within a certain proximity to the required age) can sometimes greatly negate some of the downsides to its use.

Qualitative versus Quantitative Metrics

In much the same way as binary management systems can have unintended consequences, the improper use of quantitative and qualitative data can also lead to frustration. Consider goal-setting and performance evaluations. Qualitative goals, such as "improve customer satisfaction," are important because the complexity of those topics can't be distilled down to a single number, or even many numbers. But because they can't always be easily measured, qualitative goals lack the clarity and simplicity of quantitative goals, and this can cause confusion and frustration among employees who may not be sure what they need to do to succeed. While boiling satisfaction down to a single KPI like a Net Promoter Score has some value given its measurability, it doesn't provide insight to a company on how to *change* the metric.

On the other hand, rich qualitative discussions with customers can lead to game-changing insights about what a company might do differently – but they might not be statistically significant or improve the bottom line. The key to successful use of qualitative performance evaluation is in the depth of thinking that goes into it. Cursory, qualitative evaluations provide little direction or feedback, but feedback rich with examples and suggestions can be a meaningful way to change performance.

Carrots versus Sticks

Another important systems-design choice is setting the right balance between incentives and mandates. While both can influence behavior, they do so in fundamentally different ways. Understanding the nuance of human motivation is crucial to striking the right balance. Incentives – such as bonuses, promotions, or increased flexibility – motivate individuals by offering something desirable in exchange for reaching a specific goal or adopting desired behaviors. Incentives frame success in a particular way, tapping into the desire to maximize "Me, Inc." Mandates, on the other hand, rely on authority and compliance. They prescribe specific behaviors, often with associated penalties for non-compliance. This taps into our loss-aversion bias (which holds that people feel the pain of a loss more strongly than the pleasure of an equivalent gain). Other things being equal, mandates are stronger management systems in that they more quickly shape behavior. However, they are riskier because they can breed resentment, create rigidity in the organization, and, in some cases, harden views against the behavior that is being mandated.

The basic reality is that human beings really don't like being told what to do – though the degree to which that is true, of course, varies across the population. We *strongly* prefer charting our own destiny or at least feeling like we are. Research in self-determination theory, for example, has consistently shown that people are more motivated and perform better when they feel a sense of control over their actions.[1]

When individuals are forced to do something they don't like, it triggers a psychological reaction, a feeling of having something taken away, a loss of freedom. This can lead to resistance, even if the mandated behavior is objectively beneficial.

Consider two examples coming out of the pandemic. Let's return to COVID vaccines and consider a governmental management system leveraged differently around the world – whether or not to mandate the vaccine. As with any mandate, there are always going to be strong feelings on either side. We're less interested in which side is correct than in evaluating the experiments that took place with different policies around the globe. At the time, it was very clear that the population at large held a wide spectrum of views on their desire to get the vaccine. Many were grateful and couldn't wait, viewing the vaccine as a means to get back to a sense of normalcy. On the other end of the spectrum was outright skepticism of vaccines generally. Between these extremes lay a range of perspectives, from those who were hesitant but open to persuasion to those who were enthusiastic but worried about the rapid development and testing process.

Interestingly, in populations with higher levels of skepticism, vaccine mandates often had the unintended consequence of increasing hesitancy rather than encouraging uptake. Austria provides a striking example of this phenomenon. In late 2021, faced with surging COVID-19 cases and sluggish vaccination rates, the Austrian government introduced one of Europe's strictest mandates, requiring all adults to be vaccinated. This move triggered widespread protests and a surge in anti-vaccine sentiment, with many Austrians feeling that the government had overstepped its bounds and infringed upon their personal freedoms.

The mandate didn't last long. Days before the penalties associated with the mandate were set to be enforced, the government commission administering the mandate canceled it. The brief time the mandate had been in effect had not meaningfully increased vaccine uptake in the country. Instead, it had "widened rifts in the population," the Austrian health minister Johannes Rauch said. "I am convinced that it will not help us to achieve the goal of motivating as many people as possible to have a booster vaccination in the fall. If anything, it will do the opposite."[2]

Another prickly topic coming out of COVID – and still raging – was the debate over return-to-office policies. We see a carrot-versus-stick scenario emerging here as well. Some companies opted for an incentive-based approach, offering perks such as complimentary meals, commuting allowances, or on-site childcare to entice employees back to the office. In contrast, others used mandates, stipulating that employees must be physically present a certain number of days per week and threatening consequences for noncompliance.

Although our observations are admittedly anecdotal, it appears that the incentive-driven strategy tended to foster a more positive and collaborative atmosphere at work but took longer to achieve, with lower levels of employees returning to office. On the other hand, the mandate-heavy approach got people into the office quickly, but generated resistance and dissatisfaction among employees more frequently. Neither is right or wrong – it's a question of how important speed and compliance are to the end result.[3]

The fact that mandates tend to elicit a negative response can be explained by returning to the world of cognitive science and humans' innate loss aversion. When employees were (sometimes abruptly) told to return to the office after experiencing the flexibility of remote work, many likely perceived it as a loss of freedom and control over their time and work environment. Whatever perks might have been additionally offered likely didn't outweigh the impact of that loss.

We are not advocating for defaulting to incentives over mandates when designing management systems. Sometimes the speed of change or broad compliance is paramount. For instance, mandates are widely used when the objective is safety. Think about safety-belt regulations, the mandate to watch a safety video on an airplane, or even a company requirement to have a safety moment at the beginning of every meeting to promote a culture of safety. Some things should not be "opt-in" or voluntary. In other situations, where speed may not be as important as organizational collegiality, the use of a variety of incentives might be preferred.

RELIABLE AND ACCURATE FEEDBACK LOOPS

One challenge leaders often face is gathering insights that reflect how workers truly feel and what drives their behavior. Many workers hesitate to share less-than-positive news out of fear of potential repercussions. We've both found it frustrating that, despite our repeated assurances that we want to support our team members' career growth – whether within or beyond Deloitte – people often remain reluctant to admit they're considering a move to another company, even when that move is likely to be seen as a positive step. Of course, after spending 30-plus years in the same organization, we may not seem like the most approachable figures for such conversations. But this hesitation is human nature: Sharing potentially bad news often feels risky.

An aversion to sharing bad news makes sense when you consider its likely psychological origins. In our ancestral past, being the bearer of bad news could have social consequences, leading to ostracism or even expulsion from a group. Our brains are wired to prioritize social safety and belonging, and sharing information that could be perceived as threatening to the group or its leaders can trigger anxiety and fear. It also doesn't help when a leader is known for yelling in response – talk about a deterrent to sharing bad news! Moreover, studies in neuroscience have shown that delivering bad news activates the same brain regions associated with experiencing physical pain, further reinforcing our reluctance to do so.[4]

Indeed, research by Leslie John at Harvard Business School confirms that people are prone to derogating those who tell them things they don't want to hear: We have a bias to shoot the messenger. In one of a series of experiments, John asked that participants imagine receiving news from a doctor – news that was either good (that a skin biopsy tested negative) or bad (that the biopsy revealed cancer). Participants rated their like or dislike of the physician. Sure enough, those who imagined receiving bad news liked the doctor significantly less than those who received good news. John also found that when people received bad news, they thought that the doctor had more malevolent motives and wasn't looking out for them. She posited that people can avoid the "penalty" of delivering bad news by delivering it in a certain way – specifically, by prefacing bad news by explicitly conveying the benevolence of their motives through statements such as "I love working at Deloitte and for you and I want to make you proud, but I'm thinking of leaving."⁵

Much as we might sometimes like to, leaders can't wish away human biases and irrationality. So leaders must establish feedback loops that create the preconditions for employees to provide candid, honest input regardless of the topic. Many common "employee-listening" tools – such as suggestion boxes that go mostly unused or company surveys that are met with skepticism about whether they are truly anonymous – offer limited effectiveness. That said, if the Internet has taught us one thing, it's that human beings will remove all filters if they think they are truly untraceable. This manifests in all kinds of remarkable insights and behavioral observations, good and bad. One need only compare the comment section of news sites that mandate a "real" name versus those that allow anonymous comments to see, mostly sadly, what people really think. Pejorative language is not found only in news comments – it's also found on websites where employees go under the cover of anonymity to commiserate and share information. While it's true that those using these tools represent a small subset of employees, the disparate views that are shared may indeed be representative.

Building on the observation that people become unfiltered when they are anonymous, we've found success using methods that blend anonymity with in-person discussions, fostering a culture where major issues are openly addressed and leaders can demonstrate how they handle difficult conversations. For instance, we have experimented with the use of posting publicly, but anonymously, onto a screen in a meeting large enough where the commenter could not be identified, allowing for the leader to demonstrate that tough questions are indeed welcome.

Several technology platforms facilitate this by allowing employees to submit anonymous responses visible to the entire team. This transparency helps employees see how leaders respond and builds confidence that difficult topics can be raised safely. However, this approach comes with risks. There have been many examples of leaders who have lost their cool in public, and with the pervasiveness of camera phones, these episodes may leak into the public domain. One tech CEO we advised in a company that no longer exists today had a temper tantrum in a group meeting and fired an employee on the spot, making a widely understood toxic environment even worse. Whatever management systems you design, it's important to be thoughtful about how they may be received by employees, which includes doing the preparatory work around scenarios that might arise as they're implemented.

Uninstalling Management Systems

Have a slow computer that isn't working properly? IT professionals tell us that one of the major causes is a lot of junk software building up. The central processing unit has to constantly dedicate a portion of its power to these unnecessary programs, leaving less for what you actually want to do. Junk software can also conflict with other programs or even your operating system, leading to errors, crashes, or slowdowns.

Is this analogy tortuously obvious? Yes, management systems can accumulate over time, just like junk software on your computer. People install management systems for all kinds of good reasons – rules that were put in place to solve a very specific problem that has since been resolved tend to stick around, well, forever. Sometimes these management systems don't conflict; they just take up unnecessary time and mind space.

But other times the management systems can have an unwanted negative impact on the organization's direction. In other words, they can become the *cause* of drift. A common example relates to management systems that reward financial growth, no matter where it comes from. This is a frequently used incentive for senior executives. Consider Harley Davidson, which tried to expand its customer base by offering a wider range of motorcycles, including smaller and electric bikes, only to later return to the core cruiser motorcycles and traditional customers whose loyalty fuels its brand. This type of misfire stems from incentives to grow without regard to whether that new revenue leverages the existing capabilities and management systems of the organization. When there isn't a fit, the company often struggles because they fail to adjust – or uninstall – management systems to enable the new growth vector.

> **The bad news is that the team doesn't understand the strategy.**
>
> **What's the good news?**
>
> **The strategy is already obsolete so it's better they don't follow it.**
>
> — TOM FISHBURNE

The solution to a fragmented set of management systems mirrors the solution for your computer: Uninstall what isn't working. You can't do this without visibility into all the management systems in the company, not just the critical ones. It's hard to know how they might be impacting behavior if you don't see them. When the Strategy Choice Cascade was created, the focus was on articulating just the critical management systems that were necessary to support the strategy. After decades of practice and experience with clients, especially those in large-scale organizations, we now find that it's necessary to understand all active management systems to ensure they don't unintentionally conflict with the key ones necessary to measure and manage the direction of the company. Uninstalling, or at least adjusting, the conflicting management systems is part of the discipline of honing.

Who Designs the Management Systems?

As should be evident from our discussion, the design of management systems in large-scale organizations is a complex and nuanced task. Get it right and employee behavior naturally falls in line with your objectives. Get it wrong and you can create the opposite behavior from what was intended. The stakes of management system design make it even more important to take a honing approach versus a transformation approach. Because it's not likely you'll get it perfect the first time, continual small adjustments make it more likely that you'll eventually get it right.

We've established in Part I that, when done consistently, honing an organization to keep it operating in a manner consistent with its objectives can be a less risky and disruptive approach than large-scale transformation. Transformation may be required occasionally, but it shouldn't be the first-line therapy. Honing is a terrific solution for the problem of drift, where an organization slowly stops behaving in alignment with its elemental purpose. Management systems are the tools to change the behavior of the organization to get it back on track.

It stands to reason that you might ask whose job it is to take on this challenging work. In the next chapter, the start of Part II, we'll share why we think it *must* be the CEO's job, because only they have sufficient visibility and mandate to make sure the collection of management systems create behavior consistent with their vision for the organization's direction. Deeper in Part II, we will dive into further detail on how to choose management systems that support your objectives and allow for successful honing – and share the story of a company that honed itself over the last decade. And we'll meet some other interesting artisans along the way.

Part II

HONE YOUR ORGANIZATION

CHAPTER 6

Chief System Designer

One of us had his first job as the assistant manager of a now bankrupt Canadian video store chain. We know, we know – it sounds like the setup for a bad '1990s stoner flick. But the truth is, those long shifts surrounded by thousands of movies carried an important lesson. With little else to do between customers (and there weren't that many), the days were spent consuming film after film. Unintentionally, a cinephile was created – someone who would marvel at how a tangle of words in a screenplay could be alchemized into pure magic. Steve was that accidental cinephile, at least for movies between 1980 and 1999.

Cinema is an artform whose great products are truly more than the sum of their parts. Think about a movie like *Sideways* – on the surface, a film following two generally unlikeable middle-aged men roadtripping to wine country shouldn't be a movie. But the authenticity of the location, the dialogue in the screenplay, and the performances of actors like Paul Giamatti and Sandra Oh created three-dimensional characters that audiences could connect with. Equally memorable are the duds. Consider *Ishtar* – a movie that came out amid high anticipation only to become one of the biggest flops of all time. Despite featuring two highly paid, award-winning lead actors (Dustin Hoffman and Warren Beatty), the film became more known for its cost than its quality. Abundant resources alone can't rescue a poorly designed film.

Over time, Steve started to notice patterns in what separated the bombs from the masterpieces. He could point to many films that had one standout element, yet still fell flat overall. Think of the beauty of the production of *Waterworld*, or the story and star-studded cast of *Bonfire of the Vanities*, or the old-west cinematography of *Heaven's Gate*.

At the same time, there were plenty of movies that didn't necessarily awe audiences with a single element but were captivating as a whole – *Little Miss Sunshine*, for example. The acting is solid but not showstopping. The cinematography is functional. The script is well-written but not groundbreaking. Yet the film's warmth, humor, and heartfelt message create a truly memorable experience. Or *Clerks*. Despite being extremely low budget and shot in black and white with basic cinematography, it has achieved the ranks of the classic. Or dare we put the unforgettable *Shawshank Redemption* in this bucket? When broken down into component parts, the movie contains fairly standard cinematography, a run-of-the-mill plot (there are plenty of movies about innocent people who are incarcerated), solid but not overly flashy acting, and a well-told though not particularly innovative story. Yet the movie as a whole is a deeply moving experience. Its enduring appeal lies in its emotional power, its themes of hope and redemption, and its overall sense of warmth and humanity. It just works, and people love it.

Now, these are our (well, Steve's) opinions on these specific movies; every reader likely has their own examples. The point is this: To succeed, films need to create something magical. The person responsible for this? The director.

The director's job is to pull together all the elements on the set and tinker with them in post-production until the movie is just right. Watch a great film and you forget you're watching flickering light on a screen. Time passes quickly. Inevitably, the director will leave their own stylistic imprimatur on the final product, from the slow, deliberate pacing of Stanley Kubrick, to the heart-pumping action and unique dialogue of Quentin Tarantino, to the unrelenting realism of Kathryn Bigelow. Watch a bad film and you're painfully aware of the flaws rather than immersed in the story. Worse, you're on your phone passing time.

Filmmaking demands a rare blend of skills. It requires not only the honing of one's own creative chops but also the ability to coordinate and direct a diverse team of craftspeople so that they bring their own unique artistry to serve the filmmaker's singular vision. A large organization is a lot like a film set – a complex tangle of moving parts, competing priorities, and strong personalities. Just as the director is the only person who can bring all the "systems" of a film to life at once, we assert that it is the job of the CEO to be responsible for ensuring all the systems of a business work in harmony to delight customers and meet the needs of its many stakeholders. The CEO must be the *chief system designer*.

In Part II, we will delve deeper into how to best design organizational systems that motivate behavior. In this chapter, we will share our logic for why we think CEOs must view it as their job to create a coherent set of management systems, as a movie director does for a film. Chapter 7 will feature the story of an actual film director: Sam Pollard. We'll then spend two chapters on how to design systems. Finally, we will share an example from our own world of how Deloitte has honed its management systems over time to enable our position in the market. Don't worry if you're not a CEO yourself (statistically, most of us aren't). There's value to be had from understanding the process. All of this can be used in your teams to create more effective systems.

The CEO as Chief Systems Designer

It's easy to say the CEO *should* be responsible for many things that seem vital or urgent. Given the fact that the CEO is the most senior member of the management team, it's common to hear arguments made about why the CEO must be responsible for all kinds of critical organizational imperatives. But there is one thing they *must* be responsible for. If the CEO delegates too much responsibility for systems design, it will ultimately fail.

There are three core reasons why the CEO must be the chief system designer. First, the CEO is responsible for the vision and direction of the organization. Therefore, they should be intimately aware of the organization's goals and can judge whether the organization is on course or drifting. Second, the CEO is the only person in the organization with both the authority and the visibility to create a coherent set of management systems that facilitate the collective behaviors that move the organization toward its goal. Finally, the CEO is in a unique position to both inject healthy tension and help resolve it. Productively resolving tension is a source of great innovation. Let's examine each in turn.

Setting the Destination

The CEO needs to be the chief systems designer because she is ultimately responsible, with the board's approval, for its core objective(s) and the outcomes the organization is looking to create. The CEO frames "what good looks like" for the organization. As a result, she is best positioned to judge whether the system is creating the outcomes required at sufficient speed. The CEO is also best positioned to change the objectives if and when they become obsolete. There is something unique about the clarity that CEOs must have on the direction in which they are taking their companies. With a vision for where the company is headed, the CEO can determine which actions drive in that direction and which are divergent. The notion of speed is also important. When Deloitte US's current CEO, Jason Girzadas, took the helm, he shared with us that in his listening tour with other CEOs, he received the advice that the CEO is the only person who can dictate the speed at which the organization moves. Speed is usually determined by the pace at which management systems can operate or change. Therefore, if the CEO needs to speed up or slow down the pace at which the organization is moving, she needs to have a hand on the controls – that is, the management systems.

Creating Coherence

Nothing gums up the works like management systems that promote behaviors that counteract each other. Like an eight-person rowing squad, if the oars aren't aligned, the boat doesn't move at the intended speed and in the intended direction. The CEO has two characteristics that make her perfectly suited to ensure coherence. The first is obvious: She has the authority to make any call regarding which management system(s) should be prioritized. As the senior-most decision maker, she is able to make and overturn decisions as needed. She can adjudicate when systems may be working at cross-purposes or not working sufficiently in concert.

And sometimes she may decide to reconstruct the boat (or organization) altogether. Zhang Ruimin, the CEO of Haier Group, a multinational home appliance and consumer electronics company that has grown into a global juggernaut, thinks so:

Leaders of other enterprises often define themselves as captains of the ship, but I think I'm more the ship's architect or designer. That's different from a captain's role, in which the route is often fixed and the destination defined. For example, in the past, our destination was to build the enterprise into a walled garden. Today, however, our destination is [better thought of as] a rainforest [or a self-adaptive ecosystem], and our strategy and structure have changed. And perhaps in the future we'll need to reconstruct the entire ship for a completely new route.[1]

One of the tools to create coherence while negotiating changes is visibility. Unless the chain of command is wildly obfuscated, the CEO should have a line of sight to all parts of the organization and its management systems. In many large organizations, other senior executives see a considerably narrower slice. They are far less likely to be aware of all the ways behavior is motivated. Therefore, the CEO is in a unique position to spot inconsistencies. One CEO we work with regularly conducts multi-level "skip" meetings where he meets with employees who are not his direct reports to ascertain how things are going in the middle of the organization. The CEO knows this meeting is a valuable source of insight into how the systems being implemented are manifesting outside his office. It's a terrific way to enhance overall visibility into how the system is working deep in the organization. For CEOs who have retail locations (or any kind of dispersed network of locations), there is nothing better than seeing how the system is manifesting "on the ground" by visiting a store.

Inserting and Resolving Tension

Third and finally, the CEO needs to be responsible for system optimization because doing so often requires the resolution – or healthy exploitation – of tension. Organizational tension is not a bad thing. In fact, creatively resolving tension is a key driver of innovation. Why? Because when you can resolve tension between two seemingly opposing views without merely compromising, you typically get a substantially better result.[2] Only the CEO should determine where the organization's tension should be resolved versus allowed to linger. Sometimes the best act of leadership is not to intervene and to set the expectation that the organization needs to work it out for itself. The principle here is that a CEO can deliberately inject tension into an organization to achieve a goal (e.g., to increase creativity), but they and only they are in a position to determine whether the goal has been achieved.

Consider the example of what can go wrong when a CEO does not take on this responsibility. We know of one Fortune 100 company where the CEO was concerned that the company had become too insular and operated in an echo chamber. He told his business leaders to "inject more of the outside world." Remember, a CEO's declarations and questions constitute, in themselves, a management system that can have far-reaching consequences.[3] For the CEO's subordinates, one of the easiest ways to bring in outside perspective was to start hiring more external advisors. Eventually, the CFO saw the rise in expenses and declared her own mandate (an opposing informal management system) that stated that all contracts above $100,000 for external advisors needed to be approved by her personally.

Not surprisingly, the CFO's mandate put a chilling effect on getting outside perspective. But the organization – and the consultants – adapted. Procurement started guiding management and vendors to design work to fit under the $100,000 contract level. We then observed a proliferation of "mini-projects" that didn't trigger the CFO review. This created all sorts of inefficiencies – transaction costs, rotating personnel, and so on. Presumably, this was not the result the CEO (or CFO) wanted.

Only the CEO could step in here to be the tiebreaker on which objective should be prioritized – the CFO's cost-control objective or the CEO's own advice to seek more external advice. Interestingly, the CEO didn't even have to pick a priority: The tension could simply be named, and the CEO could suggest the business leaders and CFO work together to find a creative solution that didn't rely on consultants to inject outside perspective (e.g., engaging with industry associations, academic institutions, and thought leaders, or even forming internal cross-functional teams to review ideas). Unfortunately, the dysfunction persisted for too long because the CEO focused his time elsewhere after having "solved" this challenge by issuing the directive.

This example shows that being the chief system designer doesn't require the CEO to micromanage every detail. For example, the CEO could direct the CFO and other leaders to find a solution that both reduced spending on external consultants and brought in external perspectives. By setting this objective, the CEO could allow the team to come up with a creative solution. By explicitly naming both the goal and the tension, the CEO creates clear expectations for the team – what good would look like. The team can then design within those parameters.

Most readers likely won't find this perspective controversial. *The CEO has authority and full organizational visibility in addition to setting goals and making calls.* What's new here? While our view of the CEO as system designer (and as a leader who constantly hones her organization's systems) isn't in conflict with the way the role is often characterized, many CEOs today don't see this as their role. Rather, they see themselves as catalysts for change – that is, as outspoken visionaries, sponsors of transformation initiatives, and motivators of the masses. Then, after an issue is "resolved," they move on to the next big challenge and focus there. This – unintentionally – creates a higher degree of organizational drift, and once you've drifted too far, honing won't cut it. You then need to go the route of transformation, which, as we shared in Chapter 1, is often risky, expensive, and unsuccessful.

GUARDRAILS FOR DELEGATION

There will be those who suggest that the CEO can't do "everything" and naturally ask what parts of this work can and can't be delegated. The CEO doesn't need to manage every detail of the systems that shape organizational behavior, but she must be accountable for:

- Clearly articulating the design objectives (outcomes and behaviors the management systems need to create)
- Selecting and prioritizing the key management systems that will collectively create these outcomes
- Monitoring to make sure ongoing management systems are delivering the behaviors that have the best chance at creating the outcomes the CEO is seeking

We don't see CEOs as critical to designing the specific details of each management system, nor do they need to be the person with the pen designing the details of an operating model or organization design. But the CEO must own the critical choices regarding important management systems, such as what the performance management system prioritizes and how it determines promotions, the overall structure of the business (e.g., by geography, product line, or customer), the allocation of decision rights, and others. The CEO must also have a view for how these things work together to motivate behavior.

We recently had the opportunity to spend time with Paul Polman, the former CEO of Unilever. He talked about honing Unilever to make sure that it met his objective of acting as a single, purpose-driven global company focused on long-term stakeholder value. For example, Paul noticed that many employees didn't want to move from low-tax jurisdictions to higher-tax jurisdictions. This made it hard to act globally and create leaders with international experience. So he asked the organization to create a management system that made pay for similar roles in different geographies equivalent on an after-tax basis. In addition, to get the organization focused on long-term value creation, he eliminated quarterly earnings guidance. Finally, he used ambitious goal setting to frame what good looked like (e.g., percent of goods sustainably sourced, number of new consumers to serve). Even though not all his ambitious targets in the Unilever Sustainable Living Plan were met, the company made dramatic strides at a pace not previously thought possible. And all of this was done while also delivering a total shareholder return of 300% over his tenure.

The business world is witnessing a growing recognition among both investors and managers that a narrow, obsessive focus on maximizing shareholder value alone can be detrimental – ironically, to shareholders in particular. We've previously argued that taking care of all stakeholders creates more value in the long run, because the system in which the organization operates does not get out of balance. Excessive emphasis on short-term shareholder returns can lead to myopic decision-making and cost-cutting measures that undermine customer satisfaction and long-term success. Failing to take care of employees' well-being can result in turnover beyond healthy levels and the loss of institutional knowledge and capability.

As systems designers, CEOs are responsible for creating a healthy tension and balancing the needs of all stakeholders. Companies that mix nonfinancial objectives into their metrics such as exceeding customer and employee expectations create preconditions for long-term health. Satisfying customers and employees simultaneously is akin to eating healthy, working out, and sleeping properly for individual health. Since most of any company's intrinsic value is in so-called "terminal value" – essentially, an investor's expectation that the company will continue to make money in perpetuity, not just over the next few years – longevity really does matter. As such, the CEO must have a theory of which portfolio of objectives, underpinned by a specific combination of management systems, leads to *long-term* value creation.

It's important to note that CEOs (and, to a lesser degree, other C-suite executives) also have the power to address drift much more simply than junior colleagues. Have you ever received an email from a CEO? If so, how long did it take you to respond compared to a question coming from a peer? Our bet is at least two orders of magnitude faster. Alan Mulally, the CEO at Ford during its turnaround, instituted weekly business plan reviews where he always asked, "What are your current issues and what are you doing to resolve them?" This created a culture of accountability and transparency, forcing problems to be surfaced quickly, with solutions developed collaboratively.[4]

Systems Design for the Rest of Us

Some of you might be saying to yourself, *Thanks, Geoff and Steve – when I'm a CEO I'll get right to it . . . but what about the rest of us?* Don't fear – there is an important role for system design to play at all levels of your organization, including the part of the organization that you are responsible for. The biggest difference is that your system design is framed and constrained by the choices made at more senior levels in the organization.

Imagine you're a store manager at a large chain, conducting performance reviews for your team. As store manager, you are personally measured on the feedback that customers provide when they're surveyed after they've left the store. To ensure the best performance of your team, you can institute management systems with your employees to evaluate them based on how quickly they greet customers. You can also change where people are staffed to accomplish this. In other words, you always can frame what success looks like for the part of the organization's work that you are responsible for. It's just really important to make sure you are checking that your systems do not accidentally counteract the intent of systems imposed by more broad-based management systems.

The other thing you can do is help provide visibility to your CEO (and other managers who can do the same) on how management systems are working at your level and share how they are or aren't consistent with your understanding of the organization's elemental purpose. You can also share the impact that misaligned management systems are having on the organization and make the case for change. Even better – you can put on a chief system designer hat and identify and name where different management systems are creating incoherence. Somewhat frustratingly, in many cases, the decision to make change might rest above your station. But keep raising the issue in a productive way. It's important to create visibility and help the CEO, though always do so with the mindset that there might be something you are missing.

Up to now in *Hone*, we've covered the need for organizational leaders to see themselves akin to chefs who continuously realign their blades so that the organization continues to perform as designed. We discussed the danger of drifting from the organization's elemental purpose and the importance of honing to get the organization back on track. We reviewed the importance of the management system as the primary mechanism that induces the organization to behave in alignment with its elemental purpose. And in this chapter, we articulated our logic for why the CEO must be the chief system designer to make sure that the management systems in place create the outcomes that they intend.

In the remainder of Part II and in Part III, we'll more closely examine the idea of system design. What are the different parts of a system that need to be designed? We'll introduce the idea of understanding the various actors within and external to a system and how using management systems to influence their behavior can help achieve desired outcomes. We'll discuss the difference in designing systems for a single organization versus for two or more organizations coming together in a venture, a newly formed entity, or an informal collaboration. We'll also examine the unique challenges of system design when considering an ecosystem or societal set of systems.

Before that, though, we want to take another interlude to meet a master craftsman – in this case, fittingly, a visionary whose acclaimed career has been built by coaxing, cajoling, and finding other ways to motivate people around him, from close collaborators to total strangers. The American director and editor Sam Pollard's genius lies not just in his technical brilliance, but in his ability to orchestrate human connection into profound storytelling. If the CEO is indeed like a director, they would be wise to study our next subject – a filmmaker whose work penetrates to the very marrow of the American experience, revealing truths both painful and transcendent about the country's collective journey.

Chapter 7

The Director

Filmmaking is a craft that demands a rare blend of skills. It requires not only the honing of one's own creativity but also the ability to coordinate and direct a diverse team of craftspeople so that they bring their own unique artistry to serve the filmmaker's singular vision. Like CEOs, filmmakers have an array of management systems (both formal and informal) at their fingertips, though with critics' reviews and box office returns, they have very different metrics for success. Few balance these factors as masterfully as Sam Pollard, an award-winning director, editor, and storyteller whose career spans five decades and countless acclaimed works.

Raised in East Harlem in the 1950s and '1960s, Sam's filmmaking career began unexpectedly, after a detour to university to earn – of all things – a business degree. His first jobs in the industry were as an apprentice editor on feature films before he moved into documentaries. In the 1980s, his profile began rising sharply as he collaborated with renowned documentary producer Henry Hampton, initially as an editor and director on the landmark PBS civil rights documentary series *Eyes on the Prize*. Sam's meticulous craftsmanship and sensitivity to historical nuance quickly established his reputation in the documentary world.

Sam's collaborations with director Spike Lee, starting in the late 1980s, became especially influential. He edited several of Spike's seminal films, including the jazz musical *Mo' Better Blues*, the romantic drama *Jungle Fever*, and the black comedy *Bamboozled* (which received mixed reviews on release but now is considered one of Spike's most provocative films). His work with Spike culminated in their joint Oscar nomination in 1998 for the powerful documentary *4 Little Girls*, a heart-wrenching exploration of the 1963 bombing of the 16th Street Baptist Church in Birmingham, Alabama. Sam has won multiple Emmy awards for films such as *When the Levees Broke: A Requiem in Four Acts* (about the flooding of New Orleans) and *By the People: The Election of Barack Obama*. He's also been honored with a Career Achievement Award from the International Documentary Association and a Peabody Award for "chronicling the Black experience and illuminating complicated historical figures across film and television."

At 74, Sam shows no signs of slowing down, having been nominated for an NAACP Image Award in 2025 with his son Jason for *Ol' Dirty Bastard: A Tale of Two Dirtys*, a documentary about the legendary founding member of the hip-hop group Wu-Tang Clan. "When I think about his documentaries, they add up to a corpus – a way of telling African American history in its various dimensions," Henry Louis Gates Jr., the Harvard University scholar and producer of one of Pollard's films, told *The New York Times*.[1]

STARTING THE JOURNEY

We sat down with Sam in a Baltimore café, Blue Moon Too, where the walls are heavily decorated with paintings of film characters. The documentarian in Sam was clearly on display as he spent the better part of the first 15 minutes of the "interview" interviewing us. After Steve gave his introduction, Sam very skillfully probed for more details on his background and life. Amazingly, more than 90 minutes later, Sam was recalling details about Steve's story from the beginning of the conversation, demonstrating his amazing curiosity and listening skills.

Once we were able to get Sam talking about himself, we quickly discovered that, despite his decades of success in the film industry, Sam's love for cinema remains as fresh and vibrant as it was in his youth. When asked what gave him joy today, Sam said, "I still love movies. I love watching movies. I love making movies. If anything, my passion for movies is as strong as when I was 16 years old." That passion was ignited by films such as Orson Wells's *Citizen Kane* and *Angel Face* with Robert Mitchum and Jean Simmons. Even with this love, Sam started his professional life by studying marketing at Baruch College. "I aspired to the notion of the American dream and the American melting pot where you forgot you were a person of color, not a Black American, just an American. I had an idea of becoming a businessman, wearing a three-piece suit, living on Fifth or Park. But I hated every course... especially statistics. I couldn't stand it," he recalls.

A counselor introduced Sam to a new program that promoted the participation of people of color in filmmaking in the wake of the assassination of Dr. Martin Luther King in 1968. So, in 1971, he found himself going to college during the day and film school at night, spending weekends filming short films with fellow students. As an introvert, Sam initially felt uncomfortable behind the camera, and realized early on that he was not up to becoming a cameraperson. It was in the solitude of the editing room where he truly found his calling. There, he realized that the way a story was told – its structure, rhythm, and pacing – could make all the difference in transforming a good scene into a great one, or an average movie into a masterpiece. Sam had three important mentors in the early part of his career: Victor Kanefsky, who introduced him to the world of documentaries; George Bowers, who taught him how to be a professional; and Saint Clair Bourne, who instilled in him the importance of documenting the African American experience.

Naturally, we were curious about what it was like to work with the great Spike Lee. Sam said that, as a director, Spike's style was to source terrific talent and let them do their job (his own theory of system design). He had a clear vision for his projects but also knew when to give an idea space to breathe. Sam described a terrific example of Spike trusting the editing process on the set of *Jungle Fever*. Spike was also the screenwriter on that film and had inserted a planned improv scene. The centerpiece of the movie was an affair between a Black man, Flipper, played by Wesley Snipes, and a white woman, Angie, played by Annabella Sciorra. The improv scene was a discussion about the affair between Flipper's wife, Drew, played by Lonette McKee, and several of her girlfriends. A short scene, Spike initially only wrote two lines for it – the opening and closing line for Drew. He felt that a group of Black women could improvise a better scene than he could write. The product is a terrific five minutes of dialogue and the three cameras that Spike set up are edited together beautifully by Sam.

> Spike and I shot the scene about three or four times. I was excited about doing this scene because it was really taking me back to my documentary roots, where you had to sort of shape the narrative from material that didn't have initially any sort of structure. One of the great things about working with Spike was that he could be improvisational in a way that opened me up to ideas on how to piece it together.

Eventually, Sam turned to directing himself. An episode of *Eyes on the Prize* was his first directorial outing, and it got off to a rough start. He received some negative feedback early on from Henry Hampton, the executive on the project, who threatened to fire Sam if he saw more cuts like his initial takes. Sam's fear made him apply a more directive style. He focused on executing his original vision without much debate across the team.

Over time, though, Sam realized that he needed to change up the sense that his opinion (a powerful informal management system) was the only thing that mattered for his projects. He started to recognize that he also needed the best thinking from his team. Just like a CEO who wants to prevent their questions from sending staff heading down rabbit holes, Sam became strategic about what he asks, of whom, and when. "Now, I'm always figuring out and talking to my collaborators, because I want them to help me enhance my vision," he explains. "For example, I'm doing a documentary about the Lorraine Motel and Dr. King's assassination. So the first thing I do is [go] to my camera person and talk about, how do I want the interviews? How do I want to shoot them? How do I want to shoot the verité material? This is the logic behind what I'm trying to do, visually, conceptually."

When starting a new project, Sam now engages his team from the very beginning. With his editor, he has daily conversations about the desired tone and pacing of each scene. "We talk every day, we're talking about, what do I want this scene to say? How should you approach it? You know, what kind of pacing should this sequence have? When should it have music?" he says.

Sam also involves his executive producers and other key team members in the review process, dismissing the concept of the all-powerful *auteur* who jealously guards his time or energy from the commercial side of the film business. "I want you guys to look at the assembly as a team," he says of his collaborators. "We can now figure out what's next steps. What you should choose to do, what pickups do I need to do? Do I need to do additional interviews?" he explains.

This collaborative approach marks a significant shift from Sam's earlier days, when he felt the need to assert complete control. "It was always about just Sam. It's got to be the way Sam wants completely. Anybody says anything, squash him," he recalls of that time. As he's matured, Sam has come to understand the value of embracing his team's creative input. "I've evolved and matured because I understand more and more, after all the films I've done, both as an editor and as a director, that if I don't embrace my team in the creative process, it won't make for a better – and I use this term really, very seriously – it won't make for a better *product*. Because I'm not just about creating film. I'm trying to create a product that will engage people. That's my job," he says.

Listening to Your Subject

Sam's interview style has evolved as well over the years. As a young documentarian, he and his associate producer would do hours of research on the subject of an interview, preparing a list of questions that he would dutifully go through by rote. Recalling this interviewing approach, he reimagined how the earlier part of the conversation with Steve would have played out: "So, Steven, tell me about your early life. Steven, what was it like when you went to college? Steven, where are you in your life today?"

"What I learned in the process of interviewing," Sam continues, "is that it's not about just asking the questions." He expands:

> It's about listening to the answers. So, what I began to do over the years was to always have my sheet, but to be always . . . listening for the subject to say something that wasn't one of your questions. Then you can pick up on it and say, 'Oh, but by the way, Steven, when you were telling me about working at that video store, who were the people in that video store? What was it like? What was an everyday experience?' That wasn't part of my [list of questions], but it's something new that would engage you to open up and be more human.

Sam says he's also learned how to manage the obtrusiveness of the camera in his interviews, which can change the dynamic of an interview unless the filmmaker takes steps to put the subject at ease.

> My attitude is always to make you feel comfortable. We'll talk, kibbitz. Stop, start – I'm not regimented. Sometimes I won't use the camera if [the subject is] nervous. I might say, listen, I'm just going to put my phone on. Let's just talk. I know I can always find something, because when you're editing documentaries, everything you have is the raw material that can lead to creating something wonderful. You just got to be very proactive.

Sam's warmth and curiosity about humans and their motivations and experiences shone through our interview. By the end, it felt like we had known each other for a long time. But perhaps the most important lesson we took away from Sam is that to properly hone your craft – over a career that now spans 50 years – it's not enough to just love the *output* of your craft, but you need to love the *process* of your craft most of all. If all you love is the output, you'll never put in the necessary work to become and stay great.

Sam's last message for us is that love of process is a critical input to effectively honing a craft over the years. You have to constantly return to first principles: What works for the audience? How might we make this better? If you don't love the process of making micro-improvements over time, you won't put in the work that's required and the outcomes won't come. We hear the same about athletes – those who have long, successful careers are the ones who just love to put in the necessary work. And we can imagine the same with business leaders. Those who create value in the long term for all their stakeholders are the ones who consistently return to what is going to delight customers and what behavior change needs to happen to get closer to that goal.

> Everyone loves the outcomes, but it's the love of the process that gets you the outcomes because you're willing to put in the work. I went back recently and watched the opening of three of my films that Steven Wechsler cut and re-appreciated the beauty of each. [One was] *Sammy Davis Jr.*, which was done at the last minute. [Another was] *Black Art*, which we had to completely change because nobody liked it initially. And while I was appreciating how it turned out in the end, I also found myself appreciating the process and work that went into it. If I didn't love what I do, I wouldn't put in the effort.. . . . The outcome is icing on the cake, but it's the process that I enjoy.

Sam Pollard is a paragon of craftsmanship in an industry where vision and execution must seamlessly intertwine. What truly distinguishes his approach is his profound curiosity about people and their experiences. Like the most successful executives who stay close to their customers, Pollard understands that genuine engagement with his subjects requires constant experimentation and continuous improvement. It also requires an ability to motivate individual collaborators, so they willingly put their own artistic talents in service of a shared vision and for the benefit of the audience. The end result doesn't always "delight" audiences in the superficial sense – many of his documentaries explore difficult historical moments and uncomfortable truths. The goal isn't pure enjoyment, but rather meaningful engagement. He is always looking for ways to deepen relationships – with his co-workers, his subjects, and his audience.

Finally, Pollard's career exemplifies the value of incremental mastery. It is true that breakthroughs in cinema (like any art form) can emerge from sudden discontinuities – think Akira Kurosawa's revolutionary *Rashomon*, which upended narrative structure by showing multiple contradictory perspectives of the same event, or Jean-Luc Godard's use of mobile cameras and improvisation in his 1960 New Wave masterpiece *Breathless*. But it is also true that greatness more often emerges through persistent, steady improvement – the patient honing of one's craft. Pollard didn't become one of America's most respected documentarians overnight; he built his expertise film by film, edit by edit, over many decades.

This gradual path to excellence offers a counterpoint to business culture's fixation on transformation and disruption. Like Pollard returning to his editing room to make a scene slightly more powerful, business leaders must cultivate a love for the process of refinement – the testing, learning, and iterating that incrementally transforms good businesses into exceptional ones or allows exceptional businesses to continue to make good decisions and stay competitive. In business as in filmmaking, those who embrace this craftsman's mindset are the ones who most often create work that endures.

Chapter 8

Principles of System Design

The term "systems thinking" has become widespread in management science. But its origin is surprising and not widely known: It can be traced back to a cattle ranch in Nebraska in the 1920s. That's where the son of two homesteaders, Jay Forrester, grew up – a background he later credited with cultivating his practical mind. The restless young rancher didn't stay rooted in prairie soil for long. Instead, he found himself transplanted to a bustling laboratory in Kendall Square, in Cambridge, Massachusetts, where he discovered – and then transformed – the way we think about complexity itself.

Forrester was a true genius; complex systems always came easy to him. By the time he was a young MIT researcher in the 1940s, he was already tinkering with control and information systems for military equipment, and he invented an amazing array of innovations that have had profound impact on the world as we know it today. For example, the laboratory that he was part of created MIT's first general-purpose digital computer. He also devised and patented an early version of RAM computer memory. And he led a division of MIT's Lincoln Laboratory, which created computers for the North American air defense system from the later 1950s to the early 1980s.

But there was one type of system that Forrester found particularly befuddling: human systems. Thanks to the management roles that Forrester held at MIT's labs, he discovered that contrary to popular belief, managing people was more complex than advanced engineering. He observed that, unlike physical systems, human systems are shaped by feedback loops, time delays, and interconnected elements that make their behavior difficult to predict. Actions can have both immediate and long-term effects, often in unexpected ways, and time delays mean that the consequences of decisions may not be apparent for months or even years. Forrester found that the mental models people use to navigate these systems are often flawed, leading to unintended consequences and complicating efforts to manage change. These factors, combined with the multiple interconnected elements within social systems, make it challenging to predict the outcomes of interventions and policies.

Systems Thinking

Based on these observations, Forrester developed what eventually became known as "systems thinking." Soon after, he became one of the first professors at MIT's newly founded business school and began applying systems dynamics ideas to business challenges. The rest, as they say, is history.

Before we get too far out over our skis, we recognize that we're about to use the term *system* in many different ways and we want to be as precise as possible. You've already heard us use the term *management system* to refer to the infrastructure that an organization puts in place to enable its strategy. This is the lever that the CEO as chief system designer can use to modify human behavior in the organization. We'll try not to refer to the collection of management systems as a *system* to avoid confusion, though they do operate in concert with each other with characteristics of an interconnected system.

When we use the term *system* on its own, we will adhere to its common definition. The *Merriam-Webster Dictionary* defines a system as "a regularly interacting or interdependent group of items forming a unified whole." We think that works. And as far as we can tell, that definition covers pretty much everything. From groups of atoms and molecules to something as enormous in scale as the solar system, the reality of life is interconnection. Organizations are, by their very design, systems of human beings who create outcomes via their behaviors. By definition, noting that something is a system does connote that there must be some boundaries to what is in the system and what is outside the system. For example, organizations are systems, and there is clearly a boundary between the inside and outside of an organization. But defining the organization as a system doesn't imply that it isn't impacted by things outside the organization, external to the system. It is just a way of creating some logic for the boundaries.

For ease of reading, we will try to be specific regarding which "system" the management systems are trying to impact. And if we ever need to use an entirely different meaning of systems (e.g., IT systems), we'll make sure to add in the modifiers so you know what we are referring to. Throughout Part II, we'll treat businesses as systems that require effective design. In Part III, we'll broaden the system to include multiple organizations (i.e., "ecosystems").

Back to Professor Forrester. Much has been written on systems since his original observations almost 70 years ago, and the topic appears to be particularly *en vogue* at the moment. In its simplest form, systems thinking is just the acknowledgment that solving a problem sometimes requires looking at the whole of something instead of any individual part. In business, it's valuable for tackling complicated challenges such as supply chains – the complex network of organizations working together to move a product from its origin through various stages of development to its final destination (a true "system"). It's also valuable in its application to transformational projects, which require many stages, different players, and interim milestones to achieve a lofty, long-term goal.

Systems Thinking Is Just Thinking

We're hearing more about systems thinking now than we have ever before – perhaps because it's now easier to directly see the interconnectedness of things. Consider the COVID-19 pandemic, which highlighted the world's interconnectedness in multiple ways. First, the rapid global spread of the virus itself demonstrated how easily a pathogen could travel in our hyper-connected world. Second, the "infodemic" of both accurate information and misinformation about the virus underscored how technology can quickly disseminate ideas, for better or worse. Third, the unprecedented level of global collaboration and data-sharing allowed scientists to develop effective vaccines in record time.

We think many people can get just a little bit too precious when they haul out the topic of systems thinking, noting it as if it's a new concept that's just been developed or somehow only relevant today. Our least favorite mushrooming of the idea is the gag-inducing "system of systems" (though we will admit that it's highly likely each of us is guilty of having uttered those words at some point). Many people refer to systems thinking to sound smart about a fundamental and basic reality: *There is no alternative to systems thinking.* In other words, there is virtually nothing in the world today that does not operate as a system and therefore systems thinking is just . . . thinking. Systems – or, more specifically, the interactions between many elements of a problem – exist whether or not we want to incorporate them into our thinking. For years, many people in a variety of fields tried to wish away complexity by ignoring interconnectedness (beyond corporate management, we've seen it in international affairs, public health, food production, and so on). But this didn't make the systems disappear; it just led to oversimplified analyses and ineffective solutions.

We are fans, however, of recognizing where complexity exists, even if we cannot resolve it. The Aral Sea disaster of the mid-twentieth century stands as a stark example of environmental devastation resulting from a lack of systems thinking. Soviet-era agricultural policies initiated approximately 100 years ago prioritized maximizing cotton production in the arid regions of Kazakhstan, Uzbekistan, and Turkmenistan. This led to massive diversions of water from the Aral Sea's primary feeder rivers, the Amu Darya and Syr Darya. Crucially, policymakers failed to consider the interconnectedness of the region's water cycle, ecosystem, and human livelihoods. The singular focus on agricultural output disregarded the long-term consequences of depleting the Aral Sea, triggering an ecological catastrophe that led to its dramatic shrinking and increased salinity and pollution. This, in turn, led to biodiversity loss and dust storms carrying toxic substances that caused severe health problems for local populations.[1] While most businesses do not have obvious connections that could cause a catastrophe on the order of the Aral Sea, the possibility of far-afield follow-on consequences for action should not be dismissed. We think it's far better to recognize that things are indeed interconnected and impact each other, even if we can't figure out what the impact is ahead of time.

ANTICIPATE REVERBERATIONS

Simply being aware of the concept of systems thinking, or that management systems can be used to motivate human behavior, does not confer any advantage to CEOs in their role as chief systems designers of their organizations. What does matter is how the CEO uses both to hone her organization. If things in a system are interconnected, then it stands to reason that if one part "moves" in some way – either of its own volition or caused by someone or something else – then there is a likelihood of a knock-on effect causing other parts to move. We think of these knock-on effects, or consequences, as *reverberations* of an action. Understanding the potential knock-on effects or recognizing them early and honing them is critical to being able to effectively design a collection of management systems that work well together.

Are there more such reverberations now than in the past? There is certainly a widely shared belief among commentators that, partially because of technology and partially because of the globalization that has occurred over the last half century, the world is more interconnected than ever before. Therefore, it stands to reason that leaders need to consider a higher number of potential knock-on effects that could take place when they make moves to influence the outcomes of a system – and be prepared for a larger number of exogenous shocks that will influence their own organization. However, it might also be the case that the world isn't any more interconnected than it was previously – but that we are more *aware* of the interconnectedness because of technology and the ability to observe the pattern.

Either way, good leaders need to consider these knock-on effects as they make decisions. Intra-organizationally, technology has enabled better linkages and visibility between functions and business units. For example, a manager in product development needs to be aware of how design choices might impact manufacturing costs, supply-chain logistics, and marketing strategies. Failing to consider these interconnections can lead to delays, cost overruns, product failures, or even more catastrophic outcomes.

Interorganizationally, the need for systems thinking is even more acute, as organizations must collaborate to tackle increasingly complex problems. Enabled by technology and supported by sophisticated contracting and risk-management mechanisms, these interorganizational systems reflect the realities of operating in a world with diverse stakeholders, geopolitical risks, intricate supply chains, and rapid change. For instance, a company that is sourcing materials from multiple countries must navigate a web of supplier relationships, logistic challenges, regulatory requirements, and political risks. Any disruption in one part of the system can quickly cascade throughout the entire network.

> That carrot seems more motivating than this gift card.

— TOM FISH BURNE

The escalating reliance on technology, particularly AI and automated decision-making systems, magnifies the importance of meticulous system design. In contrast to past eras where human oversight could mitigate unforeseen consequences, today's interconnected systems often operate autonomously. Trading algorithms, supply-chain-management software, and even personalized content-delivery systems make countless decisions per second, based on preprogrammed logic. This automation accelerates processes and enhances efficiency, but it also amplifies the impact of design flaws. If reverberations and unintended consequences haven't been thoroughly anticipated, the system can propagate errors at an alarming rate. For example, a poorly designed social media algorithm, intended to maximize user engagement, might inadvertently promote harmful misinformation. An AI-driven trading tool trained to maximize profit might react to unusual market changes in an unanticipated manner, generating significant financial losses. Or an autonomous vehicle's AI, programmed to prioritize speed and efficiency, might struggle to interpret unusual or ambiguous traffic situations, increasing the risk of accidents and demonstrating the imperative for robust, fail-safe design in safety-critical automated systems. As the world's AI capacity increases, attention should be paid to not just the opportunities it opens up but the unintended consequences it may have.

Lessons from the Game Room

On one of the walk-and-talk sessions that we used to create content for this book, the two of us discussed the nature of reverberations and how best to manage them, and it occurred to us that pretty good analogies can be found in the worlds of both billiards and chess. Admittedly, we kind of suck at both games – but we hope the examples will still resonate, even if they were not formed from a place of personal strength.

In the average game of pool played by average or subaverage pool players, the balls are lined up, some attempt at aiming is undertaken, and the shot is executed. A player uses the cue to strike the cue ball toward other balls with the intent of having something happen, ideally sinking one of the player's object balls into a pocket. The plan either goes well or it doesn't, in which case the player loses the right to take action for some period of time.

A novice often uses the tactic of lining things up, striking as hard as possible, and hoping for the best. A more competent player will plan a shot not just for the immediate consequence, but with an idea of setting up the next shot presuming they're going to sink a ball. The most expert player thinks ahead by three or four shots – or more – sometimes running the table and ending the game in a single turn. Using an innate understanding of geometry and physics, combined with many hours on the table learning the realities of cause and effect, expert players manage reverberations to their advantage. Experts on their "home turf" table have a leg up because no two pool tables are exactly alike. Like chefs in a foreign kitchen, sharks in a foreign pool hall are at an inherent – albeit often slight – disadvantage. They need to constantly adjust (or hone) their aiming technique, pace of shot, and degree of aggressiveness as they learn the new environs. But irrespective of the degree of difficulty, the best billiards players are able to carefully consider multiple implications of each of their moves, whether that means setting up their next several shots or snookering their opponent.

Expert chess players go a step further. To be sure, they have incredible computational abilities – they can calculate 20, even 30 moves ahead. But chess is too complicated for the human brain to master through sheer computation; the possible permutations of a chess game outnumber the estimated number of atoms in the universe. Instead, the best human players develop an intuition for the potential energy of each move, even if its ultimate effect is too far away to calculate. It is not uncommon for "kibitzers" at world chess finals – the name given to expert commentators, themselves all grand masters – to not even consider the moves made by the world's best players until they see them and realize they are perfect, often for reasons they can't quite articulate. Perhaps it is for this reason that, early in his career, the current generation's greatest chess talent, the Norwegian Magnus Carlsen, earned the moniker the Mozart of Chess. "It's hard to explain," Carlsen once told a journalist for *TIME* magazine. "Sometimes a move just feels right."[2]

So let's take this back into the world of management and leadership. Inexperienced (or less competent) leaders come into unknown situations and are prone to take "bold action" – often after careful consideration of orthodoxy, playbooks, and analysis – and hope for the best. Sometimes it works; sometimes it doesn't. More competent managers rely on pattern recognition and an understanding of the behavioral tendencies of the individuals they are trying to influence so that they can anticipate at least the first-order reverberations of an action. As they grow in competency, they will come to anticipate and intentionally provoke consequences two or three steps down the line. This notion of "leverage" – that an effect can be accomplished disproportionate to the original effort – is critical in considering where and how to intervene in systems.

The expert manager will do all this while considering a wider array of plausible reverberations, based in part on an oft-innate understanding of fundamental drivers of human behavior. They will also know that while it might be possible to plan a theoretical sequence of moves, rarely do things go exactly to plan, especially when human beings are involved. They will have a plan B or plan C in mind as an alternative means to achieve a goal if one or more moves run slightly askew. They will use a mix of small moves (when uncertainty of outcome is high or when having options in subsequent moves is critical) and large moves. They will inspire confidence by committing to the outcomes (i.e., calling their shots) when they are certain. And they will constantly hone their management systems to keep moving forward in the face of uncertain outcomes and to achieve intended consequences in line with the organization's elemental purpose. Perhaps this is the three-dimensional chess that people speak of.

Complexity Multipliers in System Design

In Chapter 9, we will lay out a continuous process that leaders can use to determine how to leverage management systems to change behavior. Before we get there, we do want to share two further observations about designing systems.

The first observation is that systems with heterogeneous behavioral motivators are considerably harder to design than those with more homogeneous motivators. The second is that the tendency for organizations to prefer predictability and low-tension environments makes it harder to incorporate continuous learning into system design because any comfort with uncertainty gets managed away. We'll examine each briefly to close the chapter.

Heterogeneous versus Homogeneous Behavior Motivations

The basic process for system design we will lay out in the next chapter is to figure out what behavior you want to change and then design management systems that motivate the behavior of the people in the system. We discussed in Part I that human behavior is motivated primarily by a desire to be successful based on how success is framed inside the organization and what is important to the individual (e.g., money, progression, work–life balance, power). The more diverse the segments of people within a system – each with their own definitions of success – the harder it becomes for the leader to implement management systems that motivate all segments equally. This is one of the reasons start-ups often find it easier to drive toward a focused goal. For the most part, everyone in a startup understands that success is defined as some "monetization" event, and they understand the (mostly) bimodal nature of the economic payoff. It's easy to define management systems that work in this kind of environment. However, as organizations scale, they need to attract more individuals. Not all new hires will have the same ownership mindset (in part because they may not receive large equity stakes). So it becomes harder to maintain alignment.

We would forgive the reader if they were to naturally conclude that we are arguing that organizations made up of people with homogeneous motivations are somehow better; that's not the case. We have devoted quite a bit of our writing in the past to the benefits of "cognitive diversity" on teams. Many studies demonstrate that successful organizations embrace a wide range of perspectives, brought by people from varied backgrounds, collaborating on teams. However, to get the benefit of having diverse perspectives, you must create a collection of management systems that motivates behavior from multiple populations effectively. No easy task.

Large universities provide a relatively simple example of the challenge of managing diverse needs and perspectives.[3] The former chancellor of the University of California at Berkeley, Clark Kerr, suggested in a tongue-in-cheek manner that a university president has three achievements to secure: "sex for the students, athletics for the alumni, and parking for the faculty." In reality, of course, it's more complicated than that. Take the faculty. Most universities evaluate professors based on some combination of teaching and research, though many lean heavily toward rewarding research. Excelling at both is genuinely difficult, yet tenure-track professors are typically required, often begrudgingly, to demonstrate competence in both areas to advance. Interestingly, the University of California system has been working on creating more defined career paths for faculty who excel in teaching. This involves establishing titles and promotion criteria that are distinct from the traditional research-focused track. The evaluation system will put greater emphasis on teaching effectiveness, student feedback, and curriculum development.[4] With this change, the university is innovating in a way that allows a more varied set of incentives for its heterogeneous stakeholders.

The Gravitational Pull of Predictability

The second key complication in system design is the tendency for organizations, as they grow in size, to have much stronger preferences for predictable outcomes and low degrees of tension and/or conflict. Management teams love predictability – more so, we'd argue, than they love great outcomes. Avoiding unexpected and unintended consequences – that is, managing risk – is an age-old management challenge. Ironically, the management systems that have been used historically to prevent unexpected consequences are the very ones that create risk of drift today. A rigid set of rules, executed without room for adjustment or even thinking, makes it hard to be nimble when things don't go as planned. Think back to Chapter 5 and the DMV employee Michelle encountered who rejected her corrected visa. When an organization's culture isn't nimble enough to try something different when something unexpected happens, it limits experimentation, learning, and innovation.

What do we mean by management systems that value predictable outcomes over "better" outcomes? Think of call centers that evaluate teams on average call time versus the resolution of the customer's issue. Or factory production lines that emphasize units produced versus those factories that give workers the autonomy to stop the line to correct errors. More nuanced systems recognize the need for multiple kinds of outcomes, not just those that can be predicted in advance. And it's not only at the point of production or customer interaction. More often than not, senior executive teams focus narrowly on meeting Wall Street expectations rather than communicating transparently about the range of potential outcomes inherent in the pursuit of long-term value creation. When this desire for predictability meets the human tendency to prefer interactions low in tension and conflict (think of the tendency to declare "We had a great meeting" simply because there was no disagreement), often the lowest-common-denominator choice wins.

Pixar is a great example of a company that has created management systems to promote candid conversations in meetings and thus be more comfortable with complexity. We've both had the good fortune to do storytelling training with Andrew Gordon, a former Pixar animator, who shared examples of their management systems that promote candor. They use an approach called "plussing" where, when giving feedback, staff identify something they like and offer a constructive suggestion to take the concept further. They also have "brain trust" meetings where films in development are regularly reviewed by peers. And importantly, they are frequently willing to go back to the drawing board with their ideas to make sure the product is of high quality, irrespective of timelines. This was done most famously with the film *Ratatouille*, which meaningfully changed direction (and directors) midstream and went on to win the Academy Award for Best Animated Film in 2008.

Pixar's innovative management systems may not apply to all companies, however. How can a company generally prevent a downward spiral toward more predictable outcomes? The key is to set the expectation that management systems aren't permanent fixtures and will change over time. Organizations can also elevate responsibility for changing and "uninstalling" management systems to the most senior positions of the firm. And they can make a point of conducting regular reviews of key management systems to make sure they are having the intended effect. These moves will give more direct control to the CEO and their team, creating better visibility into how reverberations are felt throughout the organization. The more directly a CEO observes how their actions affect employee behavior, the better they can refine those actions over time to achieve desired outcomes.

In the upcoming chapters, we will explore systems of increasing complexity, where anticipating and managing reverberations becomes progressively more challenging. We begin in Chapter 9 by examining how leaders can effectively match their interventions to their intended outcomes, applying insights gleaned from our decades of experience as growth strategists. Central to this discussion is the recognition that organizational change, like growth, hinges on individuals making different behavioral choices – someone, somewhere, must decide to change their behavior if an organization is to change. The art of modern leadership lies in discerning where to intervene, with whom to engage, and which management systems to deploy to catalyze this shift.

Chapter 9

A Recipe for Change

Before Geoff and his wife, Martha, became part-time residents of New York, he long enjoyed his visits to the city and the opportunity to hang out with Steve. Beyond the fascination with watching a dyed-in-the-wool Manhattanite interact with the mass of humanity that is the city, he knew he was in for certain experiences. He was sure to hear about Steve's latest health obsession, along with whatever new device he had acquired to monitor some aspect of his existence. He was sure to be spirited away to some impossible-to-find cocktail bar and plied with fanciful drinks. And above all: He was sure to eat exquisitely well at some place where Steve was a regular or, occasionally, an investor.

The Goldbachs briefly had an investment in a highly rated restaurant in New York's East Village in the late 2000s. The restaurant, the Tasting Room, was a 26-seat establishment opened in 1999 at the corner of First Avenue and First Street (or as Kramer from *Seinfeld* put it, "the nexus of the universe"). The restaurant was owned and operated by Renee and Colin Alevras; sadly, Colin passed far too young from a form of brain cancer in 2022 at the age of 51. We remember the restaurant's offerings as being highly original for the time: small plates, a large wine list focused on American wines, including many highly nontraditional varietals. The Tasting Room had a farm-to-table focus before that was a thing. In many ways, to dine there always felt like a special occasion.

A typical visit would start with Renee greeting you at the door. She'd apologize that you might have to wait for your table as the guest before you lingered over coffee and dessert (probably the staple

"Renee's Mom's Cheesecake"). But she would make sure you felt welcome, pouring you a glass of white wine while you waited outside on First Street. There definitely wasn't any room to stand inside the restaurant – the four-burner kitchen was in the basement and the wine cellar was in an alcove over the dining room. Once seated, a typical table would order six or seven small plates to share. A party of four could just order one of everything on the menu. A story from Renee would accompany every course that was served.

The food was magical, earning one star from *The New York Times* and 27 points for food from Zagat, the diner-rated guidebook, which ranked it among the top 20 restaurants in the city. Eric Asimov, a *New York Times* food critic, wrote in his 2022 obituary of Colin:

> Ms. Alevras patrolled the dining room, exuding sunny vibes, while down below, in a microscopic subterranean kitchen, Mr. Alevras prepared the meals, creating a new menu each day depending on what he found that morning in Greenmarkets around the city. The restaurant had no gas line; Mr. Alevras made do with an induction oven, a rare sight in a restaurant then or now. A natural tinkerer and mechanic, he built his own sous vide system, a method for cooking at very low temperatures, from parts bought on eBay. He did the plumbing and the wiring.. . . Mr. Alevras might serve a venison carpaccio that would arrive at the table coincidentally just as a supplier was carrying a whole deer through the dining room.[1]

It's safe to say that the restaurant had a cult following. In 2006, Colin and Renee decided to expand to a new, larger location on Elizabeth Street. The new location would allow for a bar in the front of the restaurant and about 100 seated guests, up from 26 seats at the First Street location. Yet the new restaurant never really got off the ground. It opened in 2007, giving it a short time to get its footing before the financial crash of 2008, when restaurants lost many patrons. And something was lost in translation. Colin was still slaving away in the now larger kitchen and those of us who dined there regularly will tell you that the food was no different, but somehow other customers didn't see it that way. Interestingly, the Zagat food rating for the Tasting Room fell to 22, and it was no longer included in the most popular ranking.

At the time, we had a realization – yes, the customer is always right, but the idea of separating a "food" rating from the entire experience was an exercise in folly. Just like when assessing a movie, customers struggle to objectively rate the individual components of a whole. If they like the whole experience, everything benefits. At the original Tasting Room, Colin's great cooking was augmented by Renee's amazing hospitality – and both were unexpected given the tiny space. Customers' overall experience enhanced their view of the food. But in the new, larger space, all the supporting elements never quite came together. (Indeed, Renee was onsite less, understandably so, having just given birth to their second child.) In *The New York Times* review of the expanded space, Frank Bruni praised Colin's food but also wrote that the restaurant "almost never had its act together during recent visits. There was waiting and more waiting: for bottles of white wine to be chilled on the spot; for dishes to be cleared; for more food to arrive. Maybe the restaurant wasn't ready to grow this much larger."[2]

Despite this failure, we feel confident stating that when Colin passed, the world lost a terrific honer. After leaving the restaurant world in 2013 to seek more financial stability, he applied his talents at Red Hook Winery in Brooklyn. "He could basically fix or figure out anything," the owner said. "A clogged drain, a labeling machine, a hi-fi amplifier, a wine with a fermentation issue – any problem, he would raise his hand and say, 'I'll figure it out.'"

The Tasting Room is a cautionary tale that shows how hard it is to just port one system into an entirely different setting. That's why transformations are risky and often unsuccessful. Perhaps with more time and no financial crisis, the restaurant could have been honed to something special and worthy of what it had originally created in the East Village. But we think that it's a clear reminder of the importance of system design and being clear on your elemental purpose when you aspire to create something magical.

The Human Factor

Just like a restaurateur must understand all elements of the customer experience – the food, the ambiance, the service, the story – a manager must be attuned to the varying needs and motivators of the people on their team. As we discussed in Chapter 6, this is especially true for the CEO, who must grasp the motivations of all the different segments of individuals within their organization. While AI has been a hot topic in recent years, with many speculating about its potential to replace human workers, the reality is that human beings remain the primary actors within all business systems. From management teams and boards of directors to unions, employees, shareholders, political organizations, customers, and regulators, the key players in any organization are, first and foremost, its people. Even AI itself is ultimately a tool designed, controlled, and deployed by human beings to serve human-defined goals.

That does not mean that groups of human beings are the only important system to pay attention to; they're just the ones that we're focused on in this book. There are, in fact, myriad other important, non-human systems that we interact with every day. We share this planet with a whole slew of other beings, and the system of biodiversity deserves our attention and respect because our existence is co-mingled with it. And beyond other life on earth, we are impacted by the cosmos that extends beyond our planetary boundaries. All of these nonhuman systems matter greatly insofar as we interact with them and cause them to change – which in turn affects human life. However, we can't "reprogram" them, at least directly. We can exert influence and natural systems will respond (sometimes), but our ability to influence is several steps – or reverberations – removed. Our ability to impact human behavior is more direct.

Behavior as Building Block

In human systems, if you want to change the outcomes of the system, someone, somewhere in that system has to change what they are doing – that is, they have to alter their behavior. This is, in effect, what honing is all about: making small changes to human behavior to alter the course of an organization toward the goal. In *Detonate*, we wrote that the most basic subatomic element of business was human behavior, and we return to that assertion here for more exploration.

Perhaps you've heard the oft-cited quote "Every system is perfectly designed to get the results it gets." The assumption here is that a "stable" system – one that consistently produces the same outcomes – is stable because the people within it behave in ways that align with how they are being motivated. Customers are buying – or not buying – based on the incentives created by companies and other forces they interact with (influencers, habits, etc.). Employees behave according to rules, norms, and other informal management systems at companies. It therefore follows that to change the outcome of a system, you need to motivate a human being – or beings – to behave differently than how they are currently behaving. This isn't a radical principle, but it's amazing to us how often it seems to be overlooked when it comes to system design. Designing good systems up front certainly makes honing them easier over time.

Back to the Restaurant: A Simple Example of System Design

To illustrate the core concepts of system design, let's return to the world of the restaurant operator as a straightforward example. While the example is simple, it's realistic both in terms of challenges the industry faces and in terms of how specific one needs to be in designing for behavioral change while anticipating reverberations.

Let's imagine a long-standing successful neighborhood restaurant in a major city. It's not too fancy – just a place with good food that locals love, though it's not a destination for many outside the neighborhood. The restaurant's customer base is longstanding and loyal. It has a small bar that also serves food, a dining area, and like many in the restaurant world, an expanding delivery business. As we open this case study, this restaurant is struggling to manage the implications of inflation in the post-COVID world. Competitive pressure has kept it from increasing prices at the same rate. Profits have therefore been squeezed, and rent continues to increase. The restaurant is relatively busy, so the owners need to be clever about how to increase profit – it's not a matter of just attracting more customers. The owners – a married couple with kids – don't want to extend their hours to add breakfast during the week to increase profit.

Yet something must change in their current business. The owners come up with an interesting solution. They decide to focus on increasing the order size of dine-in customers by encouraging the addition of an alcoholic drink or a dessert – two high-margin add-ons. As they think about how to do this, they realize that having a pre-dinner aperitif at the bar is the simplest solution; however, the bartender staff are often busy answering the phone and dealing with delivery orders. Since most of the customer base have been placing orders to go for many years, they are habituated to phoning in their orders. The owners then reason that by pushing customers to use an online ordering system, they can shift some of the focus of the staff to interacting with customers and offering them a drink while they wait for their meal to arrive at the bar or to be seated if they arrive early. A simple but elegant integrated play! How to make this happen in the real world?

As we mentioned earlier, the restaurant's system is currently "stable." That means the actors in the system have no motivation to change, and therefore the outcomes remain the same. To change the outcomes, you have to change the behaviors of at least one, if not more, actors in the system. The steps the owners should take to identify how to change the outcomes of a stable system *are the same that any executive in any organization should take as they try to drive change*:

1. Identify the actors in the system.
2. Articulate the outcome you want to achieve.
3. Identify the behavior changes for the actors in the system that will produce the desired outcome.
4. Identify the motivators for behavior change for each actor or group of actors.[3]
5. Identify and act on the management systems that trigger those motivators.
6. Hone the system over time.

Before we start to dive into each step, let's say out loud what some of you might be thinking: A small local restaurant isn't the same as a large, complex multinational. But it's actually not that different. In larger organizations, you are likely to have similar dynamics – human beings with motivations. Of course, there are likely to be a greater number of segments of those humans with common motivators. As noted earlier, motivating a heterogeneous system is harder than a homogeneous one. But the principle remains the same: You need to break the complex system down into the groups of actors and understand their motivations.

Identify the Actors

Let's start with the identification of the actors in the system. An important principle of this step is to make sure we are specific in the groupings of actors. A restaurant, like any business, has a wide variety of humans impacting its operations – suppliers, regulators, health inspectors, people shouting on the street out front, and so on. In this example, we'll keep it simple and assume there are just two central groups of people in the system that we need to pay attention to – restaurant *customers* and restaurant *employees*. It might be perfectly fine to keep it at this level of simplicity if, in step four, we find that the motivators are not meaningfully different for different groups of customers or different groups of employees. However, it also might be the case that different groups of customers and employees have different behavioral motivators, so we may need to further segment the actors. For example, it might be that we need to segment customers based on their likelihood to adopt online ordering (e.g., the "adopters" like Steve versus the "Luddites" like Geoff). Different groups of employees might also exist that require different motivation to change behavior.

Articulate the Outcome and Behavioral Change

Then it's on to articulating the outcome you want to achieve. The owners of the neighborhood restaurant know that they need to enhance profit and have a hypothesis that they can do so by having existing dine-in customers add to their order, preferably a high-margin alcoholic drink and/or dessert. They envision a scenario where their front-of-house staff, freed from the interruptions of phone orders, can dedicate their time to warmly greeting customers, offering them a seat at the bar if they are early (and ensuring prompt seating if they are on time), and elevating the overall dining experience. This personalized attention, they believe, will encourage diners to linger, savor their meals, and perhaps even indulge in an extra drink or dessert, ultimately increasing the average spend per customer. To drive this overall objective, they need to *change the specific behavior of several actors*:

1. For *dine-in customers*: Encourage them to add a drink or another menu item to their order.
2. For *delivery customers who currently phone the restaurant*: Persuade them to switch to an online ordering option.
3. For *employees*: Motivate them to focus on upselling dine-in customers to add an additional item to their order.

As is evident from this example, we can already see that it's important to further segment the customers into *dine in* and *delivery* to make the behavior objective clear. Further, within delivery customers, we are only looking to change the behavior of those who are currently using the phone. We don't want to change anything about the delivery customers who already use the online ordering system.

Identify Motivators for Behavioral Change

Once the specific behaviors are identified, then we can move on to identifying motivators for each set of actors to change their behavior. When we think of motivators, we need to think of both drivers of, and barriers to, behavior change. *Drivers* are things that can cause someone to adopt a behavior – think of them as positive motivators. *Barriers* are things that get in the way of people making change. Common barriers include being unaware of an option or feeling like it's hard or inconvenient (e.g., leaving the house to work out when it's pouring outside). Many times, alleviating a barrier is considerably more powerful than activating a driver. To borrow framing from legendary behaviorist Cass Sunstein, you can either *nudge* (motivate behavior) or remove *sludge* (take down barriers to behavior). We must consider the possible motivators and barriers for each actor.

For dine-in customers: Simply being asked by a server about adding a drink or a dessert could be sufficient to get them to consider it.

A monetary promotion (e.g., discounted drinks) could also work as long as the restaurant still comes out ahead financially on the deal. If the proprietor is present, the opportunity to get to know the owner may be reason enough for certain types of customers to linger. These are just a few examples.

Actions to remove barriers can often be even more effective. For people who prefer not to drink alcohol, ordering a soft drink might carry a light stigma, which the bartender might alleviate by creating nonalcoholic mocktails. To head off customers who really dislike getting "upsold," and perhaps to engage in the upsell in a playful way, the host or hostess could pass a card to diners at the beginning of the meal with a single check box that says, "I am 100% sure I have no desire to hear about special deals beyond my meal at hand ☺." (Who would actually check that box?)

For delivery customers who currently phone in their orders: The owners have several hypotheses for why these customers have not yet switched to online ordering. First, it may just be a longstanding habit that when they want food, they reach for the telephone first. To overcome a variety of predictable barriers associated with that habit (lack of comfort with technology, lack of awareness of the app, desire to speak to a human to feel confident the order will be accurate, etc.), the owners need to provide some incentive to try a new behavior. Addressing all of these at once, especially when different people will face different combinations of barriers, seems too tall a hill to climb. So perhaps the lowest common denominator that will have the most impact is to encourage a trial of the app via a significant – but one-time – economic incentive. A free or heavily discounted meal might catch the attention of a wide swath of customers. When they land on the app, a clean user experience and a wide range of possible customization and personalization (e.g., an "order again" or "your favorites" list) might keep them coming back.

The restaurateurs should check to make sure their existing app provides a seamless ordering experience, from browsing the menu to selecting pickup or delivery. Ongoing incentives, such as discounts, loyalty points, or exclusive deals for online orders, and automated texts summarizing orders with a simple "just want to make sure we got it right" might all entice customers to switch away from phoning in orders. And showcasing positive reviews and ratings might reinforce customers' perception of the restaurant as a strong brand and keep them coming back. Any of this sound familiar?

Act via Management Systems

All these drivers and barriers help the restaurant develop a plan to change customer behavior, and so the owners push forward. In the first month, all delivery orders receive a flyer inside the order explaining how to use the app along with a code for a discount. In the second month, instead of having a human answer the phone, the restaurant uses a recording telling people to use the online app when they call, though there is still a backup of hitting zero and giving the order over the phone. If the customer uses this option, the employee on the phone asks why they didn't use the app and offers them a code for a larger discount if they try the app in the future. If a customer says that they don't understand how to use the online system, the employee texts a link to watch a tutorial video (the direct link makes it easy for the customer to find the video). Finally, the restaurant tracks the number of phone orders to ensure it declines.

For employees: The key behavior changes for this group are to offer the dine-in customers a drink as they sit down and to steer delivery customers who phone to the online ordering service. To encourage these behaviors, on-shift managers emphasize these objectives each day in the "family dinner" that the employees share before opening. The owners also introduce a stronger motivator in the form of a sales contest to see which employees can increase their average ticket size the most. As the behavior change starts to take root, it leads to a virtuous cycle. It frees up employees' time, allowing them to focus on upselling customers and pushing phone-ins to the app. As an additional incentive, the owners decide to share a percentage of year-on-year increased profits with the employees. They also provide comprehensive training on how to serve customers and sell drinks and desserts without being pushy, to make sure that customers don't experience the added attention as "sales-y."

Hone the System Over Time

The key to the initiative's success will be to measure the effectiveness of the plan as it unfolds, so the restaurant owners implement new data reports that highlight the proportion of phone orders versus online delivery orders each day, in addition to monitoring the ticket size of dine-in customers. Both are management systems. Effectively, they want to see if the changes they are implementing are indeed driving the changes in behavior they are seeking. The owners will need to carefully watch for drift – both back to prior habits after the changes have been implemented or into an entirely different behavior pattern, which would require further honing through management system adjustments. Also, it's important to note that, while increased profit is the ultimate goal, it's not likely to be visible for a bit, so the owners must watch for leading indicators that their hypothesis is proving true.

Finally, the owners must recognize that this change is not a "set it and forget it" system. They need to continuously monitor the metrics they put in place and gather customer feedback on how they are feeling about the changes. This monitoring will provide valuable insights into what's working and what needs improvement. A data-driven approach allows them to fine-tune the app (where possible), adjust incentive programs, and refine staff training, ensuring the system remains effective and adapts to evolving customer preferences and behaviors.

The Importance of Uninstalling

All management systems, whether intentionally designed or not, inherently shape behavior within an organization. As discussed earlier, it's critical not to allow defunct management systems to accumulate over time. Sometimes the highest-impact way to promote desired behaviors is to *remove* outdated or counterproductive systems rather than add new ones. For instance, early in their journey, our restaurant owners might have realized that their method of taking phone orders, where any employee could answer the phone, was hindering efficiency and customer service. By implementing a dedicated phone line or assigning specific staff to handle phone orders, they could streamline the process and free up other employees to focus on improving the dine-in experience.

This illustrates the power of management system "uninstallations" – identifying and eliminating unnecessary bureaucracy, redundant steps, or misaligned incentives. By critically evaluating existing systems and processes, leaders can often unlock hidden potential, empower employees, and create space for innovation and growth.

> I'm not sure our management systems are configured for speed.

— TOM FISHBURNE

Of course, adding new systems and modifying existing ones is also important. The key is to approach management system design strategically and holistically – not just implementing one-off solutions, but creating an integrated ecosystem of structures, processes, and policies that work together to shape behavior and drive performance. By continually optimizing this ecosystem – adding, modifying, and removing systems as needed – leaders can create an environment that enables and inspires people to do their best work and advance the organization's goals.

Change Starts Within

Clearly, not every system is as simple as our fictional restaurant. In fact, this system is probably more complex than we made it – there could be multiple different segments of customers who behave differently as it relates to moving to online ordering. There could be multiple cohorts of employees who require different training to meet the objectives. Yet the fundamental principles of system design remain the same, whether you're running a neighborhood restaurant or a global corporation. Much like our restaurant owners, CEOs must leverage their unique position to drive change within their organization as chief system designers.

The CEO's strongest lever for change in the world is *inside* her organization: She has far more ability to motivate and demotivate the behavior of employees than she does others outside the organization. She can directly impact others' behavior with well-designed management systems to promote the type of behavior she wants. For example, a CEO looking to increase customer satisfaction might implement a new training program for employees that focuses on empathy and active listening skills. This, in turn, could lead to more positive customer interactions and improved loyalty. Ultimately, the desired behavior change might be with customers or other external actors, but for the CEO/chief system designer, the most direct route to changing the outside world is first changing the behaviors of the members of her organization that cause reverberations outside.[4] The management systems she leverages to achieve this must be dynamic, adapting to the evolving needs of the organization and its environment. This requires continuous monitoring and feedback to ensure the systems remain effective in promoting desired behaviors and achieving strategic goals. But just imagine how hard that would be if the CEO does not have an intimate understanding of the desires and motivations of the people in her organization, unlike our restaurant owners.

Balancing Innovation and Stability

In their role as chief system designer, CEOs face a constant balancing act. They must assess the extent to which they can push for behavioral change within the organization to explore new opportunities and innovate versus maintaining a focus on operational stability. This tension is particularly relevant in the context of human behavior, where change can be met with resistance and uncertainty. A CEO who pushes too hard for innovation may disrupt established workflows and create anxiety among employees, while a CEO who overemphasizes stability may stifle creativity and miss out on crucial opportunities for growth. The key lies in finding the optimal balance between these two forces, fostering a culture that encourages both disciplined execution and exploration of new ideas. This requires a deep understanding of the organization's capabilities, the motivations and anxieties of its people, and the dynamic landscape in which it operates.

To wrap up our exploration of behavioral change in system design, it's crucial to emphasize the power of incremental progress. The idea of improvement through marginal gains is well-established in operations and factory management – the compounding effects of small, incremental improvements is the key to success of kaizen and many other performance-management approaches. But it also works for people management. The most effective way to drive change within an organization is by adopting an iterative approach, continuously pushing people into new habits (and eventually the desired outcome) with small, viable moves.

This "minimally viable move" strategy allows for maximum agility, enabling leaders to quickly adapt to feedback, learn from mistakes, and fine-tune their approach along the way. For example, instead of immediately implementing all the planned changes to increase profits at our neighborhood restaurant, the owners could start by simply introducing the online ordering promotion for a limited time to gauge customer response and identify any potential issues before fully committing to the new system. This approach not only reduces the risk of large-scale failures but also fosters a culture of continuous learning and improvement.

As we've seen through the example of our neighborhood restaurant, driving meaningful change within a system requires a deep understanding of the key actors, their motivations, and the levers that can influence their behavior. The restaurant owners' success hinged on their ability to identify the critical behaviors they needed to shift, and then to strategically redesign their management systems – from incentive structures to training programs to data tracking – to support and reinforce those behaviors.

But this is just the beginning of the journey. Designing effective management systems is both an art and a science, requiring leaders to delicately balance competing priorities, anticipate unintended consequences, and continually adapt as the organization and its environment evolve. It's a challenging task, but one that is essential for any leader looking to drive change.

In the next chapter, we'll examine how honing can take place over years to develop something exceptional. We'll share the story of how a large organization that we know *very* well honed its way to increased success over the last decade.

Chapter 10

Walking the Talk

We should start this chapter with a confession: We weren't totally confident we wanted to write it. We debated the idea of writing about Deloitte's journey with honing over the last decade. We (and our colleagues) do not want to present Deloitte as an example of a company that has gotten it perfectly right. We are proud of how we've grown and the success we've had as an organization, no doubt, but there are a lot of things we could have done – and still can do – better. We are not immune to some of the performance-sapping tendencies that other large organizations succumb to from time to time that we've written about in our three books. On the other hand, we are a large organization that has grown materially over the last decade – doubling our size in the United States – and lead the market in many of the services we choose to compete in. We also are frequently asked by clients (who we hope are also readers of our books) for examples of what Deloitte does. So we'll choose to go there. This story is going to disproportionately focus on the Deloitte US organization, not because of a desire to exclude the other parts of the world but because that's where we have the most detail given Steve's previous role as our chief strategy officer.

THE BACKGROUND

Deloitte's honing journey began with the advent of the Sarbanes-Oxley Act (SOX), passed in 2002 in the wake of the Enron accounting scandal. The law established the Public Company Accounting Oversight Board and expanded the restrictions on the services that auditors could provide to clients to ensure their independence in issuing an attest report.

It also imposed personal responsibility on CEOs and CFOs for the accuracy and completeness of financial reports, making them criminally liable for intentional misstatements and emphasized the importance of internal controls. This law materially impacted the business model of the time of the large accounting firms. Around this time the major firms, each of the so-called Big 4, sold off their consulting arms – except Deloitte. EY sold its consulting business to CapGemini. KPMG spun out its consulting business into an IPO, which eventually went by the name of BearingPoint. PwC sold its consulting business to IBM, creating IBM Business Consulting Services. Actually, Deloitte did try to split its consulting business, but the transaction failed and management decided to retain the two sides of the business and carefully comply with SOX by restricting services provided to audit clients (and thereby technically constrain the growth of the consulting business to only those clients who were not audit clients).

Between the time of the failed split and around 2015, Deloitte successfully grew all its businesses by aggressively pursuing a mix of acquisitions, including Monitor Group (the firm we came from) and BearingPoint (the spinoff of KPMG). Additionally, we fueled our growth by focusing on hiring professionals with diverse capabilities to create a broad portfolio of client-service offerings.

By 2015, Deloitte found itself with a broad mix of consultative offerings designed to help executives solve many different types of problems: strategy, supply chain optimization, M&A and post-merger integration, risk advisory services, marketing, ERP software implementation, human capital, financial controls, valuation, cybersecurity, and more. In addition, Deloitte still had its legacy audit and tax businesses that we were best known for throughout our 170-year history. These combined capabilities allowed Deloitte to serve clients of all types across the private and public sectors.

Given the focus on growing the portfolio of services over time, Deloitte had been following a strategy to create "four world-class businesses" – consulting, risk and financial advisory (RFA), audit and assurance, and tax. Prior to 2015, the management team had an important management system in place to promote gentle competition across the businesses that could contribute the most to the partnership.

The executive team frequently looked at a stoplight chart comparing the four businesses with different measures of market and financial performance. The strategy worked well – at the end of 2015, Deloitte had become the number-one professional service firm by revenue in the United States.

Every few years, the partnership elects a CEO and board chair, and following a 2015 transition, the leadership team at Deloitte embarked on a refresh of its strategy. Deloitte's leadership team was initially divided over whether a refresh was necessary. After all, it would seem that Deloitte's (perhaps serendipitous) choice not to split off its consultative business from its audit business in 2002 allowed it to have a lead over its competition. The other Big 4 were rapidly building back the nonaccounting parts of their practices, Accenture was increasingly looking to get into the marketing and strategy space, and the legacy strategy firms were increasingly trying to develop implementation and technology services that had larger and longer project sizes. By all measures, Deloitte had a strategy that its competitors were replicating – and we were ahead. Why change? What was the problem that we were solving with a new strategy?

During the initial discussions, one of the executives pointed out that there was a bit of a conflict in our strategy. Deloitte had four world-class business areas, but they operated mostly independently from one another. With the exception of our audit clients, which require capabilities from across the firm to complete, in 2015 collaboration across business areas on non-audit engagements was the exception rather than the norm. Despite that operating reality, we talked about the desire to have a single Deloitte brand and a single Deloitte culture, especially among our partners, principals, and managing directors – the owners and leaders of our organization. We had drifted over time toward acting like a "holding company" with some similarities to players in advertising and marketing services. However, unlike successful advertising firms, we weren't an optimized holding company that leveraged multiple brand names to position the parts of its business differently with key buyers of that service. We mostly went to market under the Deloitte brand with limited investment in "sub-brands." And while our partners and principals shared a set of economic interests, performance evaluation was conducted deep within the organization by subspecialty and business.

We were operating as a partial holding company without embracing the full flexibility that structure offers – such as strategically using different brand names or actively buying and selling businesses to reposition ourselves in the market. This left us stuck in the middle, which is never an advantageous position in strategy.

It was also clear, at the time, that our clients' problems were becoming more complex and multidimensional. We were seeing early signs of geopolitical tensions and doubt in the benefits of globalization. The cloud computing industry was emerging, regulatory landscapes were continuously evolving, and the "gig economy" was beginning to reshape talent markets. Meanwhile, questions loomed about artificial intelligence's future impact – would it transform industries or prove overhyped? Until this point, the professional services market had been largely dominated by functional or industry specialists. In late 2015, we developed four scenarios projecting the world a decade ahead, based on varying degrees of AI pervasiveness and regulatory change. Our analysis led to one clear conclusion: Under all scenarios, the challenges our clients would face would be increasingly novel and complex, and would require mashing up multiple capabilities from across our businesses. Indeed, the thinking clarified our elemental purpose – we solve client problems and create trust in the capital markets.

An Integrated Organization

We couldn't possibly launch a new business unit for each emerging client problem – though that's precisely what a holding company model would suggest. However, we also knew we had many of the capabilities that would be necessary for the problems of the future – expertise in technology, strategy, operations, tax, financial systems, economics, and cyber, in addition to people who understood the dynamics of each of the major industries as they currently existed. If we could more easily assemble all these capabilities *on the same projects* for our clients – almost as if combining LEGO® bricks – we felt we would be better positioned to serve clients.

To achieve this mix-and-match approach required us to shift our strategy and to change the behavior of a total population measured in six figures, especially our thousands of partners, principals, and managing directors. Those were the people who would drive collaboration across our capabilities on specific client projects. Our key desired behavior change was for leaders to increasingly focus on collaboration with other parts of the organization, rather than focusing solely on taking their capability to market on their own.[1]

This sounds like it should be easy, right? Just tell people to collaborate more and they will? That's what we tried at first. Our leaders are smart operators; we hoped that if we gave them a sound logic, they would just change their behavior. But old habits die hard. For years, Deloitte had prided itself on being a decentralized organization with the majority of decision rights about what to sell and how to sell it left to our leaders, who were held accountable for their results. The (good) problem was that we continued to enjoy growth, and our leaders weren't experiencing any challenges in making their goals. But this meant there was little urgency for change. Even with internal communication campaigns highlighting that the benefits of collaborating as an integrated organization led to happier clients and longer and larger engagements, we didn't see substantial change in leadership behavior in the first stage of the strategy refresh. Our partners, principals, and managing directors would say that it was great that we wanted more collaboration, and that they believed in it in theory, but when they were evaluated, what really mattered was whether they made their numbers inside their specialty.

Encouraging Teaming

We realized at that point that we needed to make stronger changes to our management systems to promote collaborative behavior. We honed our systems in a number of important ways over the next few years. Initially, we added in a qualitative "teaming" goal in each leader's goal form, where they would be evaluated on how effectively they teamed with other parts of the organization to achieve important objectives – like increasing audit quality, creating a new offering, or driving results on an account. This increased teaming behavior to some extent, but mainly in the easiest of adjacencies (e.g., strategy and marketing, or technology implementation and cyber). When we continued to delve into why collaboration wasn't growing in the way we wanted, we realized that many of our leaders had "grown up" in an organization that was very focused on individual competencies. While Deloitte was a very networked place, these leaders didn't have a sufficient understanding of all our different capabilities. So we launched a campaign to educate our partners, principals, and managing directors on all Deloitte's different capabilities with an app called "Deloitte Does That." It highlighted opportunities for collaboration based on the buying patterns and issues of our clients.

All these shifts were meant to drive collaboration that was more organic in nature. In other words, when a client presented a problem, account leadership would assemble a customized team from across different business areas to address that specific issue.[2] This approach aligned with our vision of Deloitte offering a collection of LEGO® bricks that each leader could use to build custom solutions.

We also wanted to enable a more structured form of collaboration – similar to preconfigured LEGO® sets that come with a clear picture of the final product and step-by-step assembly instructions. This approach required us to identify important client issues and develop repeatable collaborative processes that could be deployed consistently across the organization.

New Management Systems

To promote this behavior, we created several new management systems. For the most important cross-cutting client issues, we established a new organizational construct called Strategic Growth Offerings (SGOs). These SGOs were implemented when we identified emerging client issues that required capabilities from multiple major parts of the organization and demanded significant investment to position Deloitte competitively before solution delivery could eventually become business as usual. We created SGOs in areas such as cloud computing, cyber security, artificial intelligence, and sustainability. We also created SGOs to enhance collaboration on long-standing client issues that already involved multiple parts of the organization, such as M&A and finance transformation.[3]

Additionally, we maintained a pipeline of "incubating" SGOs with smaller teams exploring what we hypothesized would become emerging client issues in the future. While these SGOs weren't traditional business areas in the Deloitte sense, they operated with approved, multi-year investment funding and specific financial targets for which leaders were held accountable. These leaders were also required to regularly report progress to leadership.

SGOs worked for large and pervasive client issues, but we also wanted to enable collaboration on more targeted issues that hit certain segments of our clients. We created what we called the "Industry Advantage Program," where we identified key issues facing clients within a particular industry. This allowed for the preconfigured collaboration to occur, but on a smaller scale and for a more focused set of client issues. We also created a similar program to tackle specific issues that stretched across clients from multiple sectors (e.g., Future of Retail, which touched all our clients with retail operations such as banking, telecom, consumer goods, and more).

Finally, over time, we deployed technology to support our offerings knowing that we live in a world that is characterized by the combination of human thoughtfulness and technology. In particular, we invested deeply across of all our businesses in technology to create consistency and efficiency in how we served our clients. For example, we created signature technology platforms in our audit and tax businesses to further our commitment to the quality of our core work.

The Realignment

Our leaders were clearly receiving the message that collaboration was important. In fact, feedback from them soon evolved: They wanted to collaborate more but felt that Deloitte wasn't making it easy enough to do so naturally. Our legacy business operating model continued to create obstacles and wasn't aligned to how the market was buying.

To this point in the journey, we had avoided major organizational change. Our reasoning was straightforward: No perfect or enduring operating design could magically align with our clients' continuously evolving issues. This was precisely the advantage of the "LEGO® brick" concept – it was resistant to organizational design limitations.

But it turned out that there was one important impediment that we could still address. Collaborating across businesses was still trickier than collaborating within businesses. We had done some realignment within our consulting business, shifting from competency-based structures (technology, strategy and operations, human capital) toward client issue-oriented teams (marketing and digital, enterprise performance, core business operations, etc.). However, we had not realigned the organization as a whole. We decided that what we needed was *fewer* business areas, which would make it even easier to collaborate on our client issues.

So we modernized and aligned our operating models across our three market-leading capabilities: audit and assurance, tax, and consultative services. We are currently in the early stages of that realignment, and while all organizational changes come with some challenges, because it has been widely recognized as an important move by our leaders it has gotten off to a largely smooth start.

Deloitte's Future

Have we gotten everything right? For sure not. The organization still needs to further hone a few areas. Most of our people still grow up deep within a specific business area. We could create better opportunities for professionals earlier in their career to build networks across the organization and better expose them to other areas. We also need to hone the management systems at the individual leadership level to promote collaboration even further, especially across business areas. And we need to hone our system to further incorporate generative AI into our workflow; this last one is clearly a big one.

Was all this intentional and planned? Again: no. That's not how honing works. Deloitte did not set out on a path where we intentionally faced a broad set of changes to management systems over the course of nearly a decade. But we did establish a new, broad-based objective – collaboration – which was grounded in our long-standing elemental purpose of solving our clients' most vexing issues. We started moving toward that goal, and when we began to drift away from that course, we adjusted.

To be fair and provide truth in advertising, inside Deloitte we have – and still do – use the "t" word to describe some of the changes we have made and continue to make today. It's a broadly used and understood word that (perhaps until now with this book) hasn't had a meaningfully better alternative. But the work we have done and the work that is ongoing – keeping ourselves economically competitive, making sure we deliver an amazing talent experience for our people, and, unsurprisingly, preparing for the age of AI – is in fact honing. We are not rethinking our elemental purpose and we are doing all of this in a proactive manner versus addressing something that had fallen into disrepair.

In discussing Deloitte's current change activities recently with one leader at the firm, he said, "Even if we're honing, it's still not easy!" We agree. We never said honing was easy. It's actually really hard: It requires constant attention, ongoing experimentation, and a deep understanding of the behavioral motivations of a whole slew of segments of people. But it's way harder if you don't address drift until it's become so significant that only a massive transformation can bring you back on course. We believe there to be a strong return on proactivity.

When management systems align perfectly, an organization – even one as vast and intricate as Deloitte – really starts to hum. You can feel the energy and momentum, a kind of harmony resonating throughout the organization. Or maybe that's just the way we feel – we are music lovers after all.

Truthfully, we've always been intrigued by the intersection of music and management and captivated by how great musicians and business leaders alike orchestrate talent, timing, and creativity. So imagine our excitement when we discovered that our final two artisans – musicians whose band we have long adored – approached their craft with the entrepreneurial spirit of seasoned executives (and that one of them moonlights as a start-up founder!).

The boundary between music and business blurred beautifully, opening our eyes – and ears – to fascinating new insights into the discipline of honing.

Chapter 11

The Rock Band

In the world of rock and roll, the decision about when to change key, break a chord progression, or shift tempo can be the difference between a good song and a transcendent one. It's in these moments of deliberate disruption that magic happens, and that audiences are jolted out of their expectations and into a new realm of possibility.

For the Canadian rock band Our Lady Peace – also known as OLP – a sense for how and when to embrace change and transformation has been the key to their enduring success, both musically and commercially. Over the course of three decades, they have navigated the tumultuous waters of an industry in constant flux, not just surviving but thriving in the face of each new challenge. For the two of us and for millions of other fans of '1990s alternative rock from the Great White North, they are among our proudest exports: a band who made it big at home and then went on to international fame.

At the heart of Our Lady Peace's sustained success are two masters of reinvention: lead singer Raine Maida and bassist Duncan Coutts. Together, they have watched as technology has rewritten the rules of the game, democratizing the creation and distribution of music while also presenting new hurdles. But rather than cling to the old ways, they have orchestrated the band's evolution, knowing just when to change and when to let silence and stillness speak volumes. One, Raine, has even found success as a startup founder, and has applied his experience as an entrepreneur to help OLP stay relevant in a dynamic industry.

When we spoke with both Raine and Duncan in early February 2025, they were preparing to head out on their "OLP30" tour, even though the band had technically formed 33 years earlier, in 1992. They have been at it pretty much constantly ever since and have achieved a level of rock stardom that only the tiniest fraction of musicians can even aspire to. Along with two other band members and occasional touring musicians, they have put out 10 studio albums, one live album, and two compilation albums. They have played over a thousand shows to millions of people, filled every imaginable performance space from arenas to heralded smaller music venues, sold many millions of albums, had songs that hit number one on the charts, and won numerous awards. And while we love their music, we decided to profile them because they have done something that only a small handful of groups have been able to do: They have remained relevant for over three decades because they have constantly adapted to the changing music scene, to fickle musical tastes, to an industry that has been utterly transformed, and to their own journey of musical and personal maturation.

An Enduring Purpose

OLP came out of the gates strong. Formed in Toronto in 1992, they struck their first record deal with Sony in April 1993, and put out their debut album, *Naveed*, in 1994. That record went quadruple platinum in Canada. However, they were anything but an overnight success.

Though he came from a nonmusical family, Raine discovered his love for music in his early teens while attending Ridley College, a Canadian boarding school. He speaks of obsessively buying rock CDs – from Neil Young to Springsteen's *Nebraska* album to early U2 albums and Sinead O'Connor. "It became my religion, staying up late into the night listening to them," he recalls. Raine would focus on the lyrics and became enthralled with how his favorite songwriters could "get these grand concepts into short, confined curbs." He also happened to meet Duncan at Ridley, their paths crossing briefly in a band but then diverging again when a rebellious Raine and the school's headmaster agreed it would be beneficial for both parties if Raine pursued his passion for music outside of Ridley.

Where did the germ of the duo's elemental purpose sprout? Duncan remembers a flash of insight into what he was going to devote his life to at the end of a U2 concert at Toronto's Exhibition Stadium on October 3, 1987. He was 18 years old. As it happens, a newly minted 17-year-old Geoff was at that show too and was struck by the same scene that Duncan remembers: thousands of people filing out when the show was over and endlessly singing the refrain to the song "40" – "How long to sing this song?" – as they melted back into the streets of the city. For Geoff, it was just a cool experience of what a social scientist today would call "collective effervescence." For Duncan, it was the moment his vocation became clear to him. He describes the experience as "a lightning bolt moment. I literally thought to myself, if I could be an individual musician or part of a band that could write a song that affected 60 people, like this song affected 60,000 people, that's what I need to chase." The experience was the inspiration for the elemental purpose of Our Lady Peace: "breaking down the fourth wall to create moments of connection and shared experience with the audience."

For Duncan, the bass guitar was the natural choice to pursue this purpose. As a cello player growing up, he was drawn to bass guitar's ability to lay down a harmonic and rhythmic foundation – the heartbeat of a song that resonates deep within a listener, subconsciously compelling heads to bob and toes to tap in unison. He taught himself bass and was quick to raise his hand when his old friend from Ridley came looking for OLP's next bassist in 1995. Raine's distinctive high falsetto gave Duncan the opportunity to provide the grounding low end that would allow the vocals to soar.

FROM STARTUP TO INCUMBENT

We could spend many pages chronicling OLP's meteoric rise and then the ups and downs of 30 years of making music, but it's the business side of what they have achieved that fascinates us the most. Though they don't often refer to themselves as such, they are the de facto CEO (Raine) and COO (Duncan) of the band. Duncan is unequivocal when he says that without Raine, there is no OLP, and it's clear that Raine serves as the chief system designer on all matters ranging from band members to management to musical style. Duncan has discovered his own valuable role as well. Early on he took on less enviable jobs like running merchandise or taking difficult phone calls from any number of people in their orbit. It felt fitting – the bassist stepping into the hidden but crucial subterranean work that keeps the band's momentum. "I think I've always been the type of person to put my hand in the air, to my benefit or my detriment, to say, 'Yeah, I'll try that.' . . . Being okay with failing in public opens a lot of doors to you." Both are unabashed businesspeople and have recognized from the beginning that while the product they put out is imbued with the luster of rock and roll, OLP was a startup that has grown into an incumbent over the years, adapting at every step along the way.

When the band launched in the early 1990s, it goes without saying that the music industry was a very different place than it is today. Musical groups carefully curated collections of songs – sometimes having to pick just eight or 10 from 30 or 40 candidates – to form an LP. They could make millions from album sales. The industry showed up in force to help them to do that, showering the best groups with marketing dollars, A&R (artist and repertoire) representatives, and plush recording studios. Excess came in many forms (expensive tours, over-the-top marketing, booze and drugs, and so on) and was often the reason for the demise of great bands. OLP had all of that . . . without the excess on some fronts.

But much like Flannery eventually found herself in a galley focused on her elemental purpose of cooking simple flavors with great ingredients in order to delight onboard guests, OLP have since pared back their offering and now have adopted a minimalist approach to production and touring. Much of that change was required by the overhauled economics of the business, with streaming both dominating music consumption and drastically reducing the revenue flowing down to musicians. But some of it is driven by Raine and Duncan's embrace of technological innovation and their desire to always look for what's next. They didn't make that shift all at once through some sort of dramatic transformation; it has happened bit by bit, experience by experience, as they have honed their model over time.

In one light, technology has democratized music, removing the gatekeepers from recording to marketing to distribution but requiring far more from the musician to succeed. As Raine describes it:

> When I was growing up, I became an expert in music. I could literally try just to write songs and produce. Now an artist has to learn how to be their own marketer. They have to be able to design their own merch and [find buyers]. They have to basically be their own agent until they get to a certain level. They have to fund this all themselves, and [they] have to learn how to write great songs and become better musicians. So, their bandwidth is now split by four or five other things.

To Raine, however, success in any endeavor comes down to creativity.

> What makes humans adaptable is creativity. If you're stuck in a certain way of doing things then, when businesses shift or sectors shift, you just can't make the transition. I saw this with a lot of artists, where once they lost that label support, they just weren't even able to find ways to do it by themselves, and they disbanded. But you also need to respect the balance between the critical mind and the creative mind. When you get the two things operating together, then it's a home run.

But Raine and Duncan have not completely avoided periods of drift on their journey. The pair describe the making of their album *Healthy in Paranoid Times* (2005) as one such moment. OLP recorded 45 songs in search of 12 truly great ones in a process that took more than three years (1,165 days, to be exact). "It just got really stressful," Raine told *Rolling Stone* around the time of the record's launch for an article spotlighting the band's wearying process. The moment when their record company president informed them that their recording costs had exceeded a million dollars sticks out in their minds: They had lost the plot on what it meant to be musicians and had fallen victim to the label-driven business model of camping out in an exotic locale – Hawaii in this instance – and pumping out songs so the management team could sift through them to find the biggest possible hits for the LP and for MTV. There was no chance that they would be able to make that money back given the changing finances of the industry, putting their future at stake.

The great streaming shift was a huge disruptor for OLP, as it was for all musicians. As Raine recalls, "I think our *Gravity* record debuted at number seven on *Billboard* in the US [in 2002]. That pushes the 'on' button for marketing money and MTV and touring and all these things. When that got taken away with the arrival of Napster, suddenly you have to reform and relook at your business model."

In a disrupted industry, live touring became the most important revenue stream. OLP had to figure out how to adapt their business model to reflect that. As Raine recalls, "We decided to change the methodology in terms of how we make records and how we publish our music. And we did. After that record, we made the next three records [alone] in this room in LA for pennies on the dollar relative to what we used to do, and that gave us the independence and the reset that we needed." Duncan adds: "I think we've made a career of adapting, from how we film things, to how we conceive music, to how we execute the recorded music, to how we actually physically tour, to how we structure our business."

The band has been on a constant journey of adaptation. They have moved between producers. They have paid attention to shifting musical styles and experimented, pulling in interesting observations from other bands. Raine has been willing to adapt his famous vocal style, often labeled "high nasal falsetto," and his signature vibrato, which is one of the hallmarks of OLP. As Duncan reflects, "We were always pushing boundaries in the studio to not rest. When we left our producer, Arnold Lanny, who did the first four records, we went to Bob Rock. The first Bob Rock record was called *Gravity*, and he got Raine to sing lower, in a more comfortable range . . . [which is] something [Bob] got from working with Metallica." And of course, they have had to weather the same crises that the rest of the world has, from financial meltdowns to COVID-19.

Another part of what has allowed OLP to last for so long is the interpersonal connection between members of the band, a recognition of the paramount importance of clarity of roles and expectations, respect for communication, and their empathy for one another – all hallmarks of any successful startup. Duncan reflects that sometimes the relationship with his band members can feel more intimate than marriage, especially over periods when they are on tour together for 21 straight months. That intimacy has allowed each to carve out a role for themselves in the music that is both important and fulfilling, even if they don't all get to play Raine's CEO role. And each has had to hone their style to fit into what the band has become.

When we asked Duncan what role the bassist plays in OLP, he describes an experience that he sees as somewhat unique: "[In many bands] the bass player becomes part of the foundation and then finds little moments to shine. But with riff-driven rock, you're not only foundational, but part of the big design of the building. You're not just finding your points to shine; you're shining all the time. You're standing up and shouting." OLP's style "made me recalibrate how I approached my craft."

That foundational role translates to life off stage. Though we described Duncan before as OLP's COO, there's a fair amount of HR in him as well as he manages the interpersonal relationships within the band and its extended touring and management family. "This won't come as a news flash, but most of us in the music business can be a bit quirky and mercurial. Creating a space for those types to communicate and relate to one another can be a tricky thing. I listen to all the different frequencies and try to bring them together to provide a foundation for people to be inspired to communicate both musically and literally." This has become even more important as the band has spent more time apart geographically – an experience shared by much of the rest of the world since the pandemic. "I work to make sure we take the time to connect face to face digitally or even on a call so we can see reactions or hear the inflection in someone's voice. [That's] an important element to our longevity. Especially now that we have the ability to add to each other's musical ideas from essentially anywhere in the world [and not just in a recording studio], it's critical that everyone's voice is heard."

Outside of OLP, Duncan spends much of his free time working with and producing younger musicians, which helps him bring new ideas and perspectives back to the band. And it's clear that his musical career is an ongoing journey, charting from his early days, when he had to teach himself to play piano and sing, to his more recent evolution in bass playing. For the latter enterprise, he talked about incorporating the tone-conforming, one-finger "claw" technique of Motown bassist James Jamerson, whom Duncan admiringly calls "one of the most devastating bass players you've ever heard in your life," to using a pick at the encouragement of another OLP band member, to studying classical violin lines. The goal is "when I get to those live moments where either things go awry or there's an opportunity for conversation in a spontaneous way.. . . I have a greater vocabulary with which to speak."

An Entrepreneurial Influence

Much of the adaptability of the band is surely because Raine has for a long time had a side gig – and episodically a main gig – as a tech entrepreneur. "I think around the 20-year mark [of OLP] I started to look for those creative sparks through other means, and that's where I got into tech pretty heavily," he explains. "It's not that music gets old, but it starts to become a bit of a machine. You're not looking for that exponential hockey stick growth. You're just like, hey, we just need to make sure that fans know we're out there, that we're still making records." What started as a side interest grew into a second career, which he sees as inextricably linked to – and symbiotic with – his work in OLP.

Among the variety of experiences he has accumulated over time, he has served as chief product officer at S!NG, a mobile app that allows artists to instantly mint NFTs to monetize their output. He co-founded the video-sharing app RecordMob. He has developed live-streaming platforms and SaaS geo-marketing tools and has built expertise in Web3 gaming and blockchain technologies sufficient to advise other companies. All of these give him a creative outlet and put him in a position where he might run across an insight that he can take back to his "other job" of being a rock star. We asked Raine to reflect on his work in tech and how it coexists with his music. "I found tech to be just as creative, in terms of conceptualizing ideas, bringing them to life," he said. "On the coding side, I'm a huge UX/UI guy. [I think] in terms of how someone touches something, how it affects their life . . . that all comes from creativity. Great CEOs are creative, in the way they manage people, but it is a muscle that you have to keep working."

The knack of thinking like a technology entrepreneur has shown Raine and the rest of the band the bright side of all the shifts in the music industry. He reflects on the value of learning from his experience with MVPs (minimally viable products) in one of his start-ups:

> The first version had some bugs: It crashed sometimes, or the interface wasn't great, so we just kept going back, and every two weeks, or every four weeks, we'd ship a new version to the App Store. It would update, and it just got better and better. Compare that with what it was like in 2012 [releasing] a song. When we released a song or an album, it was out there and that was that. There was no feedback loop you could get in front of. You couldn't go change it if they didn't like the chorus. What I learned on the tech side that we bring into the music is this ability to iterate. So yes, we release music in a much different way now. We just don't put out an album anymore. We put out a 30-second clip. You get feedback and you improve it.

This sounds to us like the very definition of honing.

Perhaps the best story of the intersection between Raine's technology entrepreneurship and the journey of Our Lady Peace comes in the form of one of his newest ventures, Fandrop. At its core, it is a geo-location-powered app designed to better connect artists with their fans, giving fans access to perks such as exclusive merchandise and in-show interactive experiences and giving artists access to their fans' contact information. Like most great products, it was born out of frustration – in this case, Raine's:

> I stand on stages every night: It's biblical for a couple hours. Then the lights go up, everyone leaves, and [the audience is] anonymous to me. All these third-party platforms, from Instagram to the ticketing companies to Myspace back in the day, they have all that data. They connect directly. The future of music really brought this inflection point where artists have to think about streaming and the revenue streams [available via data], which were away from artists. The idea for a brand-new band is to get discovered and immediately build an actual fan base that you can monetize.

Both band members bring to life the potential power of Fandrop as they imagine a variety of use cases. Duncan – ever the COO – imagines what they can do around custom merchandising, even down to personalized designs. They discovered that 62% of their fans have young kids and considered putting out OLP onesies and kid-size T-shirts. Where historically they have needed to pay 20% of the merchandise earnings to the venue, now they can sell direct to their fans. They can also start conversations with their fan base to try out new concepts. Recently, they had to course correct when they discovered that some AI-generated content in one of their song productions was not sitting well with fans and they dropped it. Another insight: They determined that a high percentage of their fans travel long distances to attend their shows, paying top dollar in a major city. Why not play at smaller venues closer to their fan base more often, lowering their production costs and making their customers happier? And so on. They have honed their marketing as well as any modern business.

And Our Lady Peace continues to evolve artistically. The last time Geoff saw them, they used holographic imagery to bring the likes of techno-utopian Ray Kurzweil to the stage. In conjunction with their OLP30 tour, they are producing a film about one of their superfans, a woman from the Bronx who has been to over 150 of their shows. They will use Fandrop along the way. As Raine anticipates:

> We play in Edmonton in a couple weeks. There'll be 12,000 people there. I'll convert 6,000 people from that crowd using Fandrop. And now those are 6,000 people in that city that I can connect to directly on our next tour or sell merch to over the course of the year. Building lifetime value with the fan has always been key to me. "Direct to fan" wasn't as important 10 years ago but the recent paradigm shift in the music business has made it critical to survival. Finding the right partners in management and promotion who understand the value of data has set the foundation for the next decade of OLP.

As we reflected on our conversation with Raine and Duncan, it again reminded us that, though they come from a seemingly different world from business, OLP has achieved something that would be the envy of any CEO. They have honed how they show up in the market through tests in logistics, organization, structure, and technology. They have thrilled their customers, to the extreme that Duncan remembers with great humility when they were once told by a fan, "I would not be alive without your music." Their members have honed their definition of what it means to be creators by taking on tasks that feed them both monetarily and psychically outside of their work in the venture. And they've managed to keep the band together (literally), to grow the business, and to be artistically productive for more than 30 years along the way. OLP is a different band today than it was in the early 1990s, to be sure: fewer crew, smaller and less equipment, video walls and holograms instead of just light shows, and so on. But at their heart, they have stayed on course, always aiming to break down that fourth wall and engage the audience.

We'll give the final words to Duncan, who summarized the points we've been trying to make in *Hone* about as succinctly as we could have hoped for: "The impetus to create encourages you to not look at what you've done in the past. For you to grow . . . you always have to push, push, push forward. Try new things. You have to [consider] new landscapes, and if you get inspired by them, then you try to incorporate that into what you do."

PART III

HONE OUR COLLECTIVE CHALLENGES

Chapter 12

Widening the Lens

Our chef friend Flannery has chosen – and honed – her career wisely. She has created a life that she enjoys for a multitude of reasons: She practices a craft that she loves, she gets to invent and experiment, she mixes up whom she interacts with on any given night, and as a sole proprietor she can say "no" when she wants to. She has control. Beyond menu and clientele choices, she chooses which knives to use for what purposes and makes sure they are always honed. This is the beauty of working in an environment where you have one ultimate decision-maker, one elemental purpose, and one set of tools to work with. Plop Flannery (or any chef) down in a communal kitchen with shared utensils, shared equipment, and varying opinions on recipes and desired outcomes and it's a different game altogether.

Our focus up until this point has been to explore *honing* within single organizations. Intra-organizational challenges are characterized by the existence of a single leader, the CEO, who is ultimately responsible for all decisions made within that organization. She has the power to act as the "chief systems designer," shaping the formal and informal structures, processes, and incentives that guide employee behavior. Up to now, we have discussed situations where there is one elemental purpose and one collection of management systems to incentivize desired behavioral outcomes.

We want to turn our attention now to applying the same concepts to multi-organizational settings where there may be a shared direction of travel but varying motivations, capabilities, belief systems, and degrees of control impacting the journey. When we first started throwing around ideas for *Hone*, one of the possibilities that got us most excited was taking solutions that we know work for individual businesses and applying them to complex multi-entity challenges. By that we had in mind not just common business examples such as forming industrial hub consortia or executing multiparty joint ventures. We wanted to apply the honing approach to gnarly societal challenges.

After laying the foundation for what interorganizational management can look like in this chapter, we will turn our attention in the next chapter to the application of the ideas in this book to the challenge of the energy transition in the face of climate change, one of the gnarliest (and highest-stakes) challenges of all.

We'll start with two core principles, though. First, we posit that as the world becomes more uncertain, multiparty solutions will increasingly become the required norm. The two of us have spent most of our careers helping organizations continue to thrive in the face of accelerating change. We keep coming back to the same conclusion: No individual company has the field of vision, data, and breadth of management systems to fully deal with inherent uncertainty. It's become clear to us that the most complex strategic challenges usually require some form of collaboration with others: other companies, other types of organizations (think: public and private sectors working together), and other people who are likely motivated in different ways.

The second core principle is that the corporate world has developed some bad habits that are spilling over into how we address larger challenges. We have trained ourselves to believe that transformation is a reliable and low-risk endeavor. We have accepted the delusion that any degree of change is possible if it is met with tenacity, shared purpose, stick-to-itiveness, and a lot of money. That is objectively not true. Transformations hardly ever work in the way intended, leaving dead careers and wasted time and money in their wake (and usually someone else to clean up the damage). So let's stop imagining that transformative effort is possible when we're trying to tackle enormous challenges like switching out our energy system. Just like we need to do in single organizations, we need to break apart even the most tangled, amorphous challenges into manageable piece parts.

> Sorry, that should have been a digital transformation.

Though more complex than operating within a single organization – and that can itself often be mind-bendingly complicated – the same basic principles apply when dealing with complex, multiparty solutions. You need:

- A direction that you are steering toward
- A clear behavioral objective for an intended audience
- An actor who can exert influence through a management system
- An ability and mindset to course correct continuously over time

As we widen our lens to consider interorganizational or "ecosystem" challenges – especially when they turn into complex societal challenges – the key is to break down complexity into these actionable pieces. And the relative effectiveness of certain types of management systems will inevitably change once you're no longer working within the four walls of an organization.

THE NATURE OF MANAGEMENT SYSTEMS IN ECOSYSTEMS

In Chapter 3, we enumerated the typical management systems deployed within organizations. It's when we start looking across organizations that things get more complicated. Management systems working across an ecosystem need to take aim not at individuals (the "Me, Inc.") but at *collective motivation*. Motivating groups is difficult, but clearly not impossible. There are three forces of gravitational pull that help different types of organizations work toward a collective outcome:

- Alignment of economic incentives
- Alignment of behavior within a legal framework
- Alignment of purpose

Thus, any management system applied in an ecosystem needs to enable or encourage alignment in one or more of these ways.

Economic Incentives. People are motivated to varying degrees by the potential not just to earn money but also through differing definitions of "success." However, at the group or ecosystem level, rational economic behavior almost always serves as a primary motivator. That's because most organizations tend to hold strong economic outcomes as the arbiter of success. In the private sector, those outcomes are typically measured by profit. But it's also true for the nonprofit world (for example, measured by efficient deployment of donations) and in government (for example, performing within a prescribed budget).

Management systems targeted at economic outcomes therefore typically involve some give and take between parties who share in the economic outcomes. Sometimes that's as straightforward as payment from one organization to another. At other times it can be a derivative or secondary form of economic value – for example, insurance to protect from downside risk or payments contingent on certain outcomes. Many books have been written on the art of negotiation and deals; we trust our readers are well-versed in that subject. As we'll discuss in the next chapter, though, we think we're too often reverting to old playbooks in considering most deals, slowing progress in ecosystem solutions due to lack of innovation.

Behavior Within a Legal Framework. As we discussed in Chapter 3, laws and regulations are the supreme management system. There is perhaps no more direct way to change individual, organizational, or societal behavior than to institute a legal requirement. When a government decides to act (or not act), it becomes *the* defining management system that directly – and often immediately – changes the behavior of all the actors in an ecosystem. Governments typically have extensive resources for enforcing regulations, and penalties for noncompliance are generally effective. Laws eclipse just about any other motivator.

Legal or regulatory "management systems" can work either as reinforcers of behavior (loans with favorable terms, grants, tax incentives, etc.) or as dissuaders of behavior (higher tax rates, fines, etc.). They can be a blunt-force instrument of law that makes individual executives liable for their actions. They can change entire businesses almost overnight, as we saw with our own experience at Deloitte following the passage of Sarbanes-Oxley (outlined in Chapter 10).

Perhaps needless to say, applying management systems within one governmental jurisdiction – where interests should, in theory, be aligned – is far more straightforward than working across jurisdictions. As the world has globalized, we are seeing the emergence of a class of problems over which no singular government entity can exercise complete control. Migration, climate change, and other planetary (and potentially, in the future, *interplanetary*) issues require the collaboration of many governments along with other actors. These are the gnarliest problems to solve because there is no single actor who holds ultimate power, as much as some might like to believe they do.

Purpose. Organizations that are motivated primarily by a purpose can in theory work with others of the same ilk to achieve a collective goal. We contend that it is very rare that alignment of purpose can outweigh economic or legal incentives, but purpose can be a contributor to action within an ecosystem. A good example is the palm oil industry, where multiple stakeholders have joined forces through the Roundtable on Sustainable Palm Oil. These stakeholders have chosen to prioritize long-term environmental sustainability, collectively agreeing to adopt practices that protect biodiversity and critical habitats, such as those essential to endangered orangutans, even when this means sacrificing short-term profits. The management system used to influence behavior in this domain essentially boils down to communication – either in the written or oral form or as demonstrated by action.

[Cartoon by Tom Fishburne: A person locked in stocks says "I feel so constrained by our management systems." Next to them, a person kneeling under a guillotine replies, "I suppose it could be worse."]

All three of these sets of management systems typically intermingle as an ecosystem organizes itself for action. No single player holds all the cards, and it is not uncommon to have some players working at cross-purposes with others. Causal relationships between action and consequence will inevitably become harder to trace as the ecosystem solution becomes more complex. This makes it harder to determine where to start and what sequence of interventions by which players and with which management systems will be optimal. But starting *somewhere* is almost always better than delaying action, tempting as it may be to simply sit back and admire the complexity of the situation.

SLIDING SCALES OF COMPLEXITY

Of course, "breaking down" complexity does not mean literally breaking the ecosystem apart. It means seeing the entirety of the challenge and the nature of the ecosystem required to address it so that a good (rarely "the best") sequence of targeted interventions can be deployed. *The more complex the challenge, the greater the number of management system interventions will likely be required to achieve a desired outcome.*

Three key factors contribute to complexity:

1. The *number of organizations* that need to be part of the solution: The more organizations, the higher the likelihood that motivations across them will differ.

2. The *diversity of organizations* involved: Different types of organizations in different industries and sectors (private sector versus government versus nonprofit) will have different objectives and will require different systems to keep them on track.

3. The *novelty of the challenge* that the ecosystem is trying to tackle: Addressing familiar challenges such as natural disaster response is simpler, as stakeholders can anticipate their roles and responses. Novel challenges, such as creating an AI regulatory framework, lack clear definitions and precedents, making it hard to foresee impacts and avoid unintended consequences.

ARCHETYPES OF ECOSYSTEM SOLUTIONS

Given the sheer diversity of ecosystem challenges, there are numerous ways organizations can work together toward solutions. We find it helpful to simplify this complexity by identifying two core archetypes of ecosystem solutions: **two-party solutions** and **multiparty solutions**. While straightforward, these two archetypes differ primarily in the number of organizations involved and the complexity of aligning their motivations.

Two-party solutions. These solutions occur when just two organizations seek mutual benefit through collaboration. Despite involving fewer players, such solutions vary significantly in complexity depending on how easily benefits can be identified and shared. Two-party solutions that offer direct economic benefit to both sides are the simplest and most common type of this arrangement. Examples include selling a kilo of steel at an agreed price, hiring a marketing agency to run a new campaign, or leasing some land from the federal government for a new infrastructure project.

The arrangement becomes more complicated when economic benefits are not immediately apparent or conventional – even if a deal is in the best interest of both sides. Such situations often require creativity or external intermediaries. For example, a consulting firm might agree to lower upfront fees in exchange for future business commitments, or a purchaser and supplier might engage in a long-term, fixed-price contract to mitigate future risks. In a different example, a pharmaceutical company partnering with an insurance provider, mediated through a third-party health analytics firm, may share patient outcome data for a certain drug. The pharmaceutical company indirectly benefits by demonstrating the efficacy and value of its medications, while the insurer gains insights to manage patient health outcomes and reduce costs.

Multiparty solutions. These solutions involve multiple stakeholders and are inherently more complex due to differing organizational motives, capabilities, and interests. Multiparty solutions typically vary based on the sectors involved and the number of jurisdictions affected. The "simplest" form of this complex archetype is when multiple organizations within the same industry collaborate, which of course needs to be done in a way that does not run afoul of any collusion laws or anticompetitive practices. In these cases, alignment typically revolves around common economic models and shared strategic objectives. However, without a central authority, these solutions often require careful negotiation to avoid competitive conflicts. Examples include initiatives to standardize sustainable packaging practices in consumer goods or collaborative safety enhancements in aviation. The US healthcare industry illustrates this complexity clearly: Hospitals, insurers, pharmaceutical companies, and patients all hold substantially different motivations despite sharing a common goal of delivering quality healthcare.

Things become more complicated when solutions must be found for organizations across different sectors within one governmental jurisdiction. Although challenging, these arrangements can benefit from potential government intervention or oversight to foster cooperation. Developing autonomous transportation infrastructure within a single city, for instance, necessitates integrating utilities, transportation agencies, private companies, and public safety advocates, all of which respond to distinct management levers.

At the peak of complexity are cross-sector, multiparty solutions across multiple jurisdictions. The diversity of regulatory frameworks, economic motivations, and cultural norms creates a significant challenge. Climate change, for example, requires coordination across numerous national governments, private enterprises, and civil society organizations – each driven by their own objectives and operating under different laws. We will examine this type of multi-jurisdictional, cross-sector collaboration more deeply in the next chapter.

A BIAS FOR ACTION

As we mentioned earlier in this chapter, and consistent with the beliefs we have espoused in our previous two books, doing *something* (via MVMs: minimally viable moves) in the face of uncertainty and complexity is almost always better than doing nothing and just admiring the problem. To return to the example of AI: It is unlikely that the best answer to how to regulate this domain is no regulation whatsoever. However, as of this writing, we don't see *any* regulation because of collective fear of getting the regulation wrong. But the thing is, we don't have to do it all at once. We *could* design a regulatory MVM, see how the market reacts, and then move again. For example, since we know that AI data centers require large and increasing amounts of energy, we could develop a framework to better match the power of a large language model with its intended use so as not to "overpower" a solution and redirect power from other possible uses unnecessarily. Some will respond positively, some negatively, and there will inevitably be some issues, but there's no better way to generate real data about potential outcomes than by taking action. The US Federal Reserve has long used a mix of active interest rate management and communication protocols as management systems to gauge market reaction: They tend to move in small increments, signaling clear intent and reasoning, to test, learn, and then act again. They are honing at each step of the way.

We understand the hesitation to act. Perhaps one way to approach the daunting nature of the challenge is to realize that we have all – on a personal level – mastered some variation of all of these archetypal challenges before. After all, as we grow from children to adults, we must manage increasing levels of complexity. If we had stopped at age six to consider the intimidating fact that entering school would require us to suddenly navigate beyond our family and include a vast network of others, we might have been paralyzed with terror (and perhaps some of us were, at first). Instead, we just grew up bit by bit, step by step, taking action where we had agency to meet increasing uncertainty over time.

Indeed, teenagers suddenly find themselves spending far more time with a group of friends than with their nuclear family – introducing new, competing dynamics within and between the two groups. When a young adult enters a romantic relationship, they must find ways to achieve common ground with their partner. If they decide to commit to one another, they are then invited into an existing family and all the dynamics that managing relations with the in-laws involve. At some point, the couple likely settles into a new community, where they must interact and collaborate with people both similar and very different from them. Finally, they grow old together and find their own and each other's capabilities dwindling, perhaps even to the point of dependency on full-time care – again a new, complicated challenge.

You see, our personal journeys parallel what we must do with complex ecosystem challenges. Just as we navigate increasingly complex social systems throughout our lives without becoming paralyzed by their scale, we can approach multi-entity challenges by breaking them down into manageable parts, deploying appropriate management systems, and taking incremental steps. We don't solve family dynamics or community issues in one transformative effort – we hone our approach with each interaction, learning and adjusting. The same principles apply to our most gnarly societal challenges: Identify the elemental purpose, focus on specific behavioral objectives, leverage the right management systems, and continuously course correct. We can do it as human beings, so we can certainly do it as leaders.

Pep talk over. We will now gather our courage and turn to how management systems and other principles of honing can be applied to, perhaps, the greatest challenge currently facing our species: navigating an energy transition in the face of climate change.

Chapter 13

Minimally Viable Thoughts: Honing Our Future

On the advice of others, both of us have recently taken up – or tried to take up – meditation. This was specifically in response to a desire to be more present and focused in our daily lives. One of us has been more successful than the other, perhaps because he listens to instructions better. That person's coach originally suggested meditating for five minutes per day. She said, "Try it out for two weeks, only five minutes." The response back to her was typical: "I think I can do more – what about ten?" She responded, "Please don't. You'll likely give up if you try and do more. Just do five." So that's what happened. And five grew to 10 over time, and only a handful of days have been missed in the last five years.

Sometimes when we look at how society is addressing the many issues surrounding energy and climate, it feels like we are trying to meditate for 20 minutes a day – or an hour, or more – from the start. Humanity is faced with an incredibly complex problem: how to power a growing world, especially with the rise of AI and the development of the Global South, while ensuring energy reliability and security *and* minimizing the worst impacts on our changing climate. This involves balancing numerous competing interests and priorities, making the challenge feel almost insurmountable. We can't wish away the complexity of this challenge – in fact, we think we need to embrace it. The only way to achieve broad enough support for any of these individual priorities is to show how they can be achieved without sacrificing progress on the others.

Before we get too far in this discussion, we want to say this first: When this challenge is raised, we feel that too often the conversation gets immediately labeled as political. We are well aware of the varying perspectives on these topics, particularly in the United States, where we reside. To be clear, we do not want this section to be perceived as articulating a political view. Instead, in this chapter, we want to share a "clinical" argument for creating systems that can help enable society to achieve these goals without the need to meaningfully compromise on any of them, a result that a plurality supports. As avowed capitalists, we believe that there is value to be created by resolving these complex needs because resolving them reduces costs, reduces risk, and has the potential to create topline growth. A final caveat: Not only do we not want to be political, but we also want to be clear that these are ideas we are sharing in the spirit of ending the book with "minimally viable thoughts," as we did in *Detonate* and *Provoke*. We are more than open to being debated or shown where we have it wrong. Our hope is that this contributes to an open dialogue to start to hone our way to better solutions.

With that out of the way, let's continue.

One thing that gives us hope and confidence is that *needing more energy* is common ground for regions, countries, and people of all stripes. We also all need more energy security, energy efficiency, energy independence, and sustainability. The key problem we observe, however, is that any solution to meet these needs is usually framed as an immense challenge that necessitates transformational, sweeping change. As anyone who's ever attempted some kind of behavior change has learned – even quotidian ones like meditating 10 minutes a day, sticking to a strict healthy diet, or getting to sleep by a certain hour – adopting new practices requires forming new habits and dislodging old ones, bit by bit, one behavior at a time. It requires building new muscles to expand impact over time. Behavior change can be very, very hard, but it can be done.

Our first suggestion is to move away from focusing on the very long term. We know that human beings have cognitive biases that massively discount the impact of things in the distant future, making behavior change driven by very long-term goals unlikely. In saying this, we are by no means suggesting that it is unnecessary to have a long-term target in mind because of the fact that we're working on planetary timeframes – it *is* necessary. It's just that we can't rely on that goal to be a reliable motivator of human behavior. And yet many sustainability professionals focus on big, overarching long-term goals like a specific emissions reduction target in the distant future. Challenges also exist with proposals that require massive human behavioral change in a short period of time (e.g., banning internal combustion engines, making plant-based meals the prime option in hospitals); these are not likely to convince a large proportion of the population to change their behavior, and backlash is a likely result. Overfocusing on revolutionary technology (e.g., commercially viable carbon capture) is a risky bet, too. These are all akin to large-scale corporate transformations, which, as we've noted, mostly fail. People tune out when they feel like the sacrifices are too onerous to sustain and they are unable to see progress because it is so far in the future. Momentum is hard to gather with this as the dominant change philosophy.

Not surprisingly, we prefer the equivalent of the five-minute-per-day-approach. What if leaders could deploy and hone management systems that would rely on gradually changing behavior in small ways to build momentum and confidence? Over time, we will learn and could make iterative changes to these management systems to continue to get the necessary behavior we need to address humanity's complex set of energy needs. This doesn't wish away the planetary timeframe; it just breaks it down into human timeframes that work from a behavioral standpoint.

Honing Complex Collective Challenges

Unlike most of the other examples we've presented, the energy transition does not involve simply managing the culture within one company or figuring out how to respond to a new technology or a few savvy competitors. Instead, the energy transition space has many different actors, each with distinct motivators, operating with different timeframes and economic realities. The point around timeframes is easy to overlook, but particularly important to keep in mind. You have multiple intertwined, unique dynamics at play with very different time cycles. Developers of new energy infrastructure (not just cleaner or renewable energy; this is broader: We also need grid, transmission, and other infrastructure upgrades) have capital-allocation timeframes that are decades long. Governments typically want to show progress in two- to six-year windows. The UN-sponsored Conference of the Parties on climate change meets annually. Investors have vastly different timeframes for when they would like to show a profit, some of them quite short-term. And the consumers of the world evaluate their purchases on a daily basis. Finally, all of this intersects with the natural world, which has its own timeframe that is immeasurably complex.

If different time scales make your head spin, consider another factor: The energy issue is a challenge that breaches organizational, sectoral, and geographical walls. It is global and requires players with wildly differing desired outcomes and motivations to work together. The motivations are as vast as the number of humans on the planet. Here, it's important that we recognize and lean into the motivations of different groups to find solutions that meet the majority of needs on a segmented basis without material compromise; the alternative is gridlock. This is why we think it's imperative to show that there does not need to be a compromise between meeting rising energy demand, doing it reliably, and doing it in a sustainable way. In fact, trying to maximize only one of these is likely to fail because actors who prioritize the others will likely block other solutions. Understanding the motivations of different segments of actors and deploying distinct management systems that change their behaviors toward a long-term goal is a better strategy than hoping the same message will work for all.

In the remainder of the chapter, we'll look at how the principles of honing can be brought to bear on this incredibly complex system. We are going to focus mostly on investing in new, clean energy infrastructure as our example. As we delve into this further, it's important to have a basic understanding of the underlying economics of this kind of investment. The upfront fixed capital costs are extremely high, and most of the money is spent before any revenue comes in. But, if successful, the infrastructure can last for a long period of time, paying out revenue and earnings over decades. This is often seen as a risky endeavor in that most of the money goes in before a dollar is returned. Compare that to simple software businesses today that have a high ratio of fixed to variable costs. It's faster to get to the first prototype, at which point you can start earning revenue, but you can easily make changes to the product to adapt to changing needs. It is harder to do that in the energy world.

It's tricky to get into the detail of potential solutions without getting into the guts of the problem. So, with apologies, we're going to get a bit wonky over the next few pages. To those of you who are not energy experts, we encourage you to go forward undaunted! We believe it's a particularly useful example for all readers, and we've tried to keep things accessible. After all, leaders in all industries and sectors are increasingly going to run into challenges that require them to act as part of a collective in which there is no central control, and they will similarly have to go deep on industry-specific challenges and solutions. What works to help make progress in the energy transition will be quite different from, for example, how to create broader access to affordable, nutritious food, but the principles on how to approach it are the same.

Follow the Money

The crux of the challenge in the energy transition is that many executives and leaders recognize the eventuality and need for long-term change.

However, muscle-memory that prioritizes short-term action overrides this awareness, and the result is inaction. Because we believe (and wrote about in the *MIT Sloan Management Review* in September 2024[1]) that inaction is a poor choice that is likely to leave companies competitively disadvantaged, we need to pursue novel solutions that get us "unstuck."

Earlier in the book we wrote extensively about the importance of motivating behavioral change, but what is the best way to do that in this context? An obvious answer – especially where institutional change is needed – is, of course, money. If economic interests can be aligned, any problem is more likely to be solvable. While not all institutions are equally motivated by economics, they all pay attention to them. Whether you're a profit-oriented company responsible to your shareholders, a public office working on behalf of your constituents and their well-being, or an NGO striving to make the best use of your donation dollars, economic outcomes are sure to come up at your board meetings or their equivalents.

In the energy ecosystem, there are scenarios in which money can play a clear catalyzing role. For example, when someone decides to put solar panels on their roof because the savings from electricity usage offset the upfront cost over time, you don't need a lot of external stimuli to make it happen. This is a straightforward case where one party acts because of direct, immediately obvious economic benefit.

For a slightly more complicated example, imagine a solar developer who has the technology and land to build a one-gigawatt (for those not in the space, that's pretty big!) production facility. The solar developer faces a lot of risk in spending their capital without knowing in advance what the demand might be or the price for their solar output. To mitigate that risk, they might look for a stable, long-term buyer, called an "offtaker" in the energy business. The offtaker and developer might enter into something called a long-term Power Purchase Agreement (PPA), which would provide price and demand certainty to both entities, reducing the risk both face from market fluctuations on the price of electricity. The trick here lies in finding an offtaker who values the certainty of supply more than the absolute price of electricity. You can easily see how a player like an AI company would be a natural offtaker for the solar developer; the AI company's need for consistent power is immense and the margins in technology are high, so they would value a long-term, consistent electricity supply at a knowable price. Forming an agreement with the AI company would help the solar developer get off the ground because the presence of a large anchor customer could give them the ability to attract smaller customers, financing, employees, and so on. In this example, two parties agree to partner because a mutually agreed-upon plan benefits both economically and strategically.

But what about situations where the immediate monetary benefit is less clear, or where there's a multi-step sequence of behavioral changes required before the majority of the system benefits? This is a pretty common condition in long-arc changes like the energy transition. The trick to getting started is understanding (a) what "building block" management systems exist to enable behavioral change, and (b) where in the sequence of behavioral changes there is likely to be a sticking point, or as we think of it, a "leverage point," where extra attention may be required to overcome critical barriers.

Making the Economics Work

There are several actors who have the power to deploy or influence the economic incentives that can jumpstart desired behavior change. These actors have at their disposal powerful management systems that can motivate behavior change across an entire sector. Admittedly, not every player in an ecosystem has equal control over management systems, and some must work to influence others rather than act directly for a desired outcome. We devoted a substantial chunk of *Provoke* to the art of, well, provoking other players in an ecosystem to do something you want them to, so we won't repeat all that now. For the purposes of making progress in the energy transition, let's assume that all players are aligned on the need to move forward, and it's a matter primarily of sequencing the right management systems to achieve the sequence of desired behaviors.

In the energy transition space, consider the following examples of how different actors can motivate change.

Governments can introduce incentives or regulations in a variety of ways that promote behavior change in a manner consistent with their policy priorities (we've previously noted that government actions are powerful management systems). Incentives can take various forms, such as loans, grants, economic backstops, or tax credits. While this is often the first mechanism that comes to mind, our observation is that these incentives are usually not nimble enough. They often require too much red tape to access, or they last far beyond the need to stimulate the initial behavioral move. Alternatively, as the "stick" to the "carrot" of incentives, governments can use the rule of law to compel action, either by making inaction economically disadvantageous or by making it illegal *not* to take action. Congestion pricing in the city of London, for instance, is an example of this kind of regulation. As we've stated throughout, government policy is probably the strongest management system in existence.

NGOs and philanthropic organizations, particularly those that are well funded, can bend economics using similar methods as government incentives such as loans, grants, and economic backstops.

Finally, **private corporations** that can benefit from shaping the way a new industry evolves may leverage their own economic stability to trade a risky short-term economic investment for the potential of a long-term payoff. For example, we see several large technology players willing to pay higher short-term costs for clean energy to power their AI infrastructure if it can guarantee that energy on a long-term basis (e.g., investments in on-site nuclear reactors, geothermal generators). As we'll examine later, Deloitte and several other companies are investing in sustainable aviation fuel (SAF) to ensure the long-term viability of the aviation industry. Private corporations usually make these choices because they see long-term value from cost reduction or predictability, risk mitigation from the decreased chance of supply interruptions, or customer demand from having a cleaner and more reliable energy base.

If you're not one of these entities, don't fret. Sometimes the best thing to do is find the entity that has the motivation and ability to create a game-changing management system and convince them to make their move.

Identifying the Leverage Point

Now let's imagine how management systems, deployed by the actors above, could chart a growth path for a subscale clean energy technology – say, clean hydrogen. As we try to imagine what an ecosystem solution might look like, we often find it easy to tell a story about how it might unfold.

Our story begins with a shared belief – across national and regional governments, players in the energy community, and consumers of energy who are looking for more sustainable solutions on top of greater supply and energy security – that getting to scale with clean hydrogen is an important objective. Here, "getting to scale" means moving from a nonexistent market today to one in the future where we have abundant supply that is easily transported and offered at a price that encourages increased adoption of new energy sources. We have the technological know-how to make clean hydrogen, and we apparently have widespread motivation. But where to start?

Barring some sort of immediate financial incentive from natural market activity, usually the most direct way to catalyze action is for a government to provide an incentive to get players to pay attention. Once you have counterparties from critical parts of the value chain (supply, demand, infrastructure, etc.) at the table – lured by "free money" from the government – then someone needs to make the first deal and establish a pilot project. That project can serve a variety of purposes: to allow the companies to get to know each other, to pressure-test the technology and other critical operational assumptions, or even just to prove to the world that it can be done.

With that pilot project complete, the government could intervene again to spark interest in other regions within the country with similar need profiles and assets. After publishing the results and conditions for success in the pilot region (and perhaps compensating the pilot players with tax incentives for divulging intellectual property), the government could use a competition-based grant program for other regions to implement the project's successful approach. The US's Infrastructure Investment and Jobs Act (or Bipartisan Infrastructure Law) of 2021 launched such an initiative with its Regional Clean

Hydrogen Hubs program, using a wide range of management systems – from subsidies to information sharing – to spur the development of a brand-new clean energy source. That story is still playing out as of this writing (April 2025) and may be quite different by the time you're reading this.

We made a number of critical assumptions to construct this story. Some may be fair assumptions under certain circumstances (e.g., that government-funded pilot-scaling programs would work) and some may turn out to be wishful thinking (e.g., that tax incentives are sufficiently compelling to encourage sharing of intellectual property). All, though, are "leverage points" where intervention from a management system to drive behavioral change – and then honing of that management system over time – can help drive the intended outcome behind the assumption and let the solution continue to develop.

The key assumption in the story above that we have found in our real-life work needs the most attention is how that very first deal for the pilot project gets done. It turns out, that's a messy problem that will not resolve itself without management system intervention.

Getting Beyond the Chicken and Egg

In our work as sustainability business leaders, we hear from organizations all the time that they would love to be part of a solution, but some other part of the ecosystem needs to shift first. That other part of the ecosystem would love to be part of a solution as well, but only under some other condition, and so on. Action is stalled as players issue a collective shrug and hope for the best for some sort of transformative change to get things moving. This is the classic "chicken-and-egg" problem plaguing many complex systems: the need to motivate someone or something to take action to catalyze the system.

In our example above, what should come first: the demonstrated ability to provide supply at a reasonable cost, the signal of demand-side offtakers willing to do a deal, or the enabling infrastructure? Good question, and the answer changes based on the stakeholder. In most real-life situations, in fact, what we see is lots of individual chicken-and-egg problems piled up on and intertwined with one another across a system; it might more aptly be described as the "systemic first-mover dilemma." In these situations, multiple potential counterparties are worried that if they move first, they may get stranded. They also worry that if they don't move soon enough, they may get left behind. And to make matters even more complicated, as we shared earlier, various management systems may be working on vastly different timelines: A government department that needs to get something done within a political leader's tenure (usually a small number of years) is quite different from many energy company capital-allocation systems that think in horizons of 20 or 30 years.

The reality is that in many new energy domains – think hydrogen, carbon capture, nuclear fusion, and so on – we're not facing a lack of technology (we generally know how to do it) or desire (we know adoption will create new playing fields, lower costs, stimulate economic activity, etc.). We simply can't get the early-stage economics to work, largely because of this "chicken or the egg" quandary. Suppliers may have the technological know-how to start to produce the clean energy alternative, but they can't get access to capital for their projects without showing financiers concrete proof that they have purchase contracts lined up. Financiers may have the "dry powder" of cash reserves or liquid assets, but they can't commit to the clean energy projects unless they're sure they can earn equal or better returns for their portfolios.

Purchasers of clean energy may be broadly motivated to enter into a contract but be averse to traditional terms that could lock them into a long-term cost disadvantage as the technology scales.

To break these stalemates, the first objective is to catalyze *someone* to move first, using a means different from simple financial incentives or idealistic government interventions. Let's assume that some sort of government incentive creates enough attention to bring possible players to the proverbial table. Then what?

CONTRACTING FOR MARKET MOMENTUM

We have established that the critical barrier to overcome is reluctance to be one of the first movers. So our most important leverage point is getting actual first contracts to be signed. As you've probably surmised by now if you've made it this far in the book (or read *Detonate*), we believe that the rote application of past "best practices" to novel problems rarely works – and this is true for contracting. Traditional energy contracts are built for more certain situations with knowable, predictable outcomes. To address new problems successfully, we must go back to first principles to identify the behavior that we want to change (someone enters a contract) and identify the barriers that exist for different segments of actors in this system to perform that behavior. As we'll see, it doesn't really take new-to-the-world thinking to nudge this system – in many cases, applying contracting concepts that have been used elsewhere can get a first contract over the hump. In the energy transition space, getting that first contract may very well be the key to spurring broader change.

But why? In the energy transition space, the key to getting to a first contract lies in precisely identifying why actors who see the long-term benefit of the transition to clean energy won't make the first move. That is how we can start honing management systems to design innovative contracts that can change behavior and spur action.

The behavioral barriers we observe are generally linked to the different types of uncertainty that actors face. Suppliers of clean energy face high initial capital costs with a long payback period, creating uncertainty on several levels: What is the price they will receive for a good (energy) that has a market commodity price? What is the overall demand for the capacity they're creating (i.e., how much of their capacity can they expect to sell?). The greater the proportion of their capacity that is predictable in terms of price and demand, the more they can just focus on the core actions of building the infrastructure and supplying energy. But even then, suppliers also face uncertainty around the operational elements (technology, production, infrastructure, etc.) coming together seamlessly when needed.

Buyers face a different type of uncertainty that is akin to FOMO – they don't want to miss the advantages of being a first mover, but they also don't want to be stuck with contracts for clean energy that are overpriced relative to the market, especially when they are enabling the market by buying early. They also don't want to pay higher prices early if they aren't somehow rewarded by getting some benefit later as demand rises and other buyers come in. The uncertainties facing investors are reverberations from the uncertainties facing suppliers and buyers: They need a balanced supply-and-demand system to work to earn a fair rate of return given the risk they are taking.

In all these cases, the good news is that we don't necessarily need completely "new-to-the-world" solutions to get over the uncertainty barriers. We just need to import solutions that have been used in other problems outside the energy space. We'll examine each of the uncertainties facing the clean energy contract space and suggest possible ways to resolve them.

Price and demand uncertainty for the supplier (and investor): A big challenge suppliers face is not knowing what the long-term market price might be for the energy they produce. Usually, especially in high-capacity plants, demand would come distributed across many potential customers. But in a new space, the producer doesn't have the ability to aggregate or even know whether there is broad-based demand for their project, let alone know what the price of the output should be. That uncertainty can be enough to prevent investment, so we are looking for ways to provide more certainty in price and demand. We have seen several contracting – or deal-making – mechanisms bridge this gap. The simplest is demand aggregation vehicles, like purchasing alliances. By combining their buying power and committing to multi-year purchases, these alliances significantly reduce investment risk for producers by guaranteeing future sales. In 2024, the Sustainable Aviation Buyers Alliance secured commitments from 20 corporate customers valued at $200 million[2] to buy high-quality SAF in advance of such fuels being produced at scale.

Auctions are a second mechanism to breaking the stalemate. This approach matches clean energy producers with buyers through competitive bidding. Sellers offer their lowest acceptable price, while buyers bid their highest. This can be an effective way of aggregating demand, quickly. We've also seen governments in some cases step in to subsidize differences between the production cost and the auction price.

For instance, the A-4 auctions in Brazil, which are designed to produce new energy generation capability, follow this approach. Not limited to just one type of renewable, government subsidies meant that auctions between 2019 and 2024 stimulated significant new capacity awards across solar PV, thermal, hydroelectric, and wind sources.

Another clever way to create more predictable demand patterns is through a mechanism known as a Contract for Differences (CfD). In these types of contracts, the buyer or seller can engage with a third-party broker to effectively guarantee a constant price for what they are buying or selling. The broker assumes the risk in price fluctuations for an upfront fee. In some cases, the government is willing to step in and act as that broker. The UK's Dogger Bank Wind Farm program, a large renewable project, due to be finished in 2027, was established using a CfD between the developer (a joint venture between SSE Renewables, Equinor, and Vårgrønn) and the UK government. Established in 2019 under a contract with three phases, each 15 years in length, this agreement ensures that if the market price is below the agreed minimum price, the government pays the difference to the developer; if the market price is above the agreed minimum price, the developer pays the difference to the government.

Operational uncertainty for suppliers is another important element to overcome. This can include whether the technology is ready when needed, whether necessary infrastructure will be available on time and at a feasible cost, or if the necessary collaborators are willing to join a complex supply chain. All of these operational uncertainties can work to prevent the initial move to invest in energy production. We have seen several mechanisms used to mitigate these uncertainties. The simplest is to insure aspects of the production timeline. Developers can purchase insurance to bridge and transfer part of their investment risk, and insurers can purchase reinsurance to protect them if a project fails. Insurance can also be purchased to cover start-up delays, construction and/or operational challenges, and environmental liability.

One specific challenge that energy project leaders face is that they require the collaboration of many parties, whose interests may not be clear. Publishing a nonbinding Expression of Interest (EoI) is a mechanism a potential leader of a new project can use to request responses from prospective partners to evaluate the viability of the new opportunity before the leader formally requests a full proposal. EoIs also allow system participants to signal their interest in collaborating. This is important to facilitate information sharing, a critical component of eventual collaboration. For example, Climate Investment Funds (CIF) issued an invitation in late 2024 for eligible countries, with their multilateral development partners, to respond to an EoI as part of its Industry Decarbonization program. The promoted benefits of the program included "CIF's programmatic approach, a predictable and flexible envelope of up to $250 million per country in concessional resources, and [encouragement of] direct involvement of the private sector throughout the process."

Finally, the "book and claim" contract addresses some aspects of both demand and operational uncertainty. In the clean energy space, buyers who want to achieve lower emission commitments don't always have direct access to nearby clean energy sources given transmission constraints. And suppliers of clean energy would prefer to have access to a market broader than where they can transmit the output of their power generation. By using book and claim contracts, sellers can reach a global market where they supply power to local consumers, but the credit for using a cleaner source of energy is "sold" to a customer anywhere in the world. These customers – not the local consumer – receive the credit for the lower emissions. Governments can use management systems to encourage use of book and claim accounting by clarifying precise methods for tracking and reporting the use of clean energy. The state of Oregon did this for renewable natural gas by clarifying its requirements, starting in 2023, for participants to use the Midwest Renewable Energy Tracking system for tracking renewable tracking certificates.

We are encouraged by the fact that all of these deal-making approaches are being played with in different parts of the energy system in various regions of the world. Each would need to be specifically honed for the deal in question, but we're confident that more widespread application – at that critical leverage point of first-mover motivation – could be one of the keys to unlocking accelerated progress in the energy transition.

Walking the Talk Part Deux: Deloitte and SAF

At the time of writing, Deloitte is part of an experimental consortium of organizations committed to driving an SAF ecosystem in Minnesota. The effort is spearheaded by an economic developmental organization, Greater MSP, to drive SAF production around the Minneapolis-St. Paul Airport. Several management systems are at work in promoting this effort. On the supply side, several government incentives are promoting the creation of an SAF industry, from a tax credit for qualifying SAF/conventional jet fuel blends to a new section of the tax code that shifts the focus to broader clean fuel production to a state tax credit to qualifying taxpayers who produce or blend SAF in a certain state. All of these add up to start to tip the economics in favor of SAF project development.

On the demand side, a number of organizations with long-term climate commitments like Deloitte are looking to seed demand for SAF because airline travel is a key component of their carbon footprint. As a result, several of them have committed to be part of a demand consortium to purchase SAF from this hub over the short to medium term to help provide stable economics to potential producers. This consortium includes Bank of America, Ecolab, and Delta Air Lines, in addition to Deloitte, and it has committed to purchasing the first several million gallons of SAF each year, starting in 2025. This is expected to help drive down the cost of making SAF. These corporate demand signals act as an important management system to give confidence to investment in production facilities.

As a result, initial production investments have been made. Delta and Flint Hills Resources are in the early stages of creating the first SAF blending facility in Minnesota and many alternative feedstocks are being considered. Delta is deeply committed to a sustainable aviation industry and is placing itself at the center of many of these ecosystems to ensure the long-term viability of the industry. As their chief sustainability officer, Amelia DeLuca, likes to put it, "Nobody should have to choose between seeing the planet or saving it." That's the essence of a no-tradeoff approach.

Much Work to Be Done

One small chapter in one small business-y book was never going to solve all the challenges of the energy transition. But we hope the time we have spent with it provides insight into how any player in the mix can map out ways to apply *Hone* principles to influence others and achieve their objectives via the application and honing of management systems. We have covered just one leverage point to overcome barriers to scale of just one clean technology, which in itself is just one small solution in the much larger set needed to make any noticeable progress in the energy transition.

But that's the point. Stop admiring the enormity of the problem and declaring long-term goals with bold transformational agendas. Instead, identify one concrete element you can influence with a management system at your disposal, take action, and move forward. Hone a bit and take another step. And another. And another . . .

Chapter 14

Reflections on a Trilogy

We had simple goals when we started this trilogy eight years ago. The primary one was to capture our experiences and observations working with some of the world's largest companies. We wanted to explain the behaviors that made them simultaneously among the most successful businesses in history, and those most threatened by disruption. We sought to enable leaders to move faster and be less encumbered by past decisions without destroying the business in the process. What we hoped to do was show that one could move fast *without* breaking the wrong things. We had no clue whether the ideas would resonate – or even whether we'd like each other after spending so much time arguing. We think we do, but we still argue. And we certainly didn't set off to write something that could be viewed in the rearview mirror as a coherent trilogy about more effective leadership in a world where previous practices aren't always a useful prologue.

The germ of this set of work can be traced back to a workshop we co-facilitated in Chicago in 2016, where we started discussing the possibility of writing something together. Steve said he had an article in mind – maybe for *HBR*, something like that. Geoff offered a guest slot on a blog he was writing at the time; Steve politely declined and said he had something a bit more ambitious in mind. When Wiley started calling Geoff looking for ideas for books based on insights from the practice he was running at the time, we decided to jump into the deep end – not knowing how to swim and without a life jacket. The first edition of *Detonate* was littered with typos that still embarrass us to this day. (We fixed them all in the second edition but there are way too many of those originals floating around for our liking.) We also learned

> This time, let's try moving fast **without** breaking things.

—TOM FISHBURNE

that it's kind of hard to sell a book called *Detonate* in airports. There aren't any specific rules making such an evocative title illegal; it's just that some booksellers have outdated corporate orthodoxies that probably need to be – well, blown up.

We knew we wanted to write books that (a) were quick reads, (b) didn't lead us to take ourselves too seriously, and (c) focused on principles of management, not playbooks. But even with those guidelines, we still debated the books' form. Geoff originally wanted to have a large coffee table book with illustrations, a nontraditional entry into what he thought was (and still thinks is) generally a boring category. Steve convinced him that perhaps our audience might want to read our book on the go and carrying around a coffee table book was impractical. Geoff pushed for being creative about enlivening the text, which brought us to the wonderful Tom Fishburne and his witty "marketoons." After we committed to an approach for *Detonate*, we received some welcome news when Lowell McAdam, then CEO of Verizon, shared that he started and finished an early draft on a flight. We were very glad that he didn't come back and say he fell asleep or preferred the movie.

REVISITING OUR BROADER PROJECT

After three books, we've learned a bunch and still have loads to learn. One lesson is that it's amazing how much better you get at communicating the core idea of your book *after* the book has been published. Once you are forced to explain out loud, multiple times, to multiple audiences, what the core idea of the book is, it reveals myriad ways the original text could be improved upon. That said, we tend to look forward and not backward, so we have no intentions of publishing an update; bereft of his own, Steve would pull out Geoff's hair if we were forced to do that! But now that we have your attention, this chapter is a second chance for us to remind our readers of the core ideas of *Detonate* and *Provoke*, perhaps one last time. Maybe this might inspire some of you to revisit them yourselves and let us know how we could tell the story differently.

We wonder a lot about the impact AI will have on the writing process and even the desire to consume books in the traditional way. Just this morning, Steve shared a podcast with Geoff on which the host described uploading a book to a large language model and then engaging with the book as he drove, instead of just listening to the text. Sounds cool! We did experiment with using AI to write *Hone*, primarily for research and to sharpen some text (see our acknowledgments for more details). Why not? The ideas are ours and we want to use all available tools to improve them where we can. We wonder, though: In the future, will readers want books about what authors want to say when they can ask AI to create personalized versions of whatever they want to hear about? How will an author earn the right to push their views on others? And if there are no authors, how will future AI be trained? There are certainly smarter and more informed people than us with answers to these questions. Still, we are curious: Can AI replace us as writers and do a better job?

Since we're endeavoring to boil *Detonate* and *Provoke* down to a few pithy points, we thought it would be fun to ask various AI tools to summarize our work. This entry was the best, we thought, in response to the question "What do Geoff Tuff and Steven Goldbach write about?"

Geoff Tuff and Steven Goldbach are business authors and Deloitte consultants who primarily write about innovation, adaptation, and leadership strategies for businesses facing disruption and uncertainty.

Their most notable works include:

1. Detonate: Why – and How – Corporations Must Blow Up Best Practices (and Bring a Beginner's Mind) to Survive *(2018) – This book challenges traditional business approaches, arguing that many "best practices" have become outdated rituals that hinder rather than help companies.*

2. Provoke: How Leaders Shape the Future by Overcoming Fatal Human Flaws *(2021) – This book focuses on how leaders can navigate uncertainty by making proactive choices rather than simply reacting to change.*

Their writing typically emphasizes:

- The need to question established business practices
- How cognitive biases affect decision-making
- Strategies for thriving in uncertain environments
- Practical frameworks for business innovation and transformation
- Leadership approaches that embrace ambiguity and complexity

Their work is particularly focused on helping organizations become more adaptable and responsive in rapidly changing business environments.

We recognize that by including this text we are also creating a time stamp of when this chapter was written (April 2025). AI's capability to answer questions like this will only get better, so it might be fun to revisit the same query in a few months when *Hone* actually launches.

That aside, it's a pretty good summary! Nonetheless, it misses some important nuances. Here's what the books were about from our own perspective, unfiltered by AI: *Detonate* is first and foremost a book about opening our eyes to the orthodoxies that pervade daily life at work, at home, and everywhere in between. Only once we recognize when we are operating by rote can we start to ignite change by breaking our learned habits. In businesses and other large organizations, this orthodoxy creates all kinds of behaviors that just don't pass the smell test.

Many of these things masquerade around organizations as so-called best practices. The problem with best practices is that, by definition, if everyone around you follows the same best practices they are no longer best. They are average. And what business leader wants to be average? The playbooks of business that have been crafted over decades yield an approach to management that is more concerned with risk mitigation than delighting customers and staying ahead of accelerating change. Many of these are so ingrained in business habits, there is no explanation for why we do things the way we do beyond "Well, that's just how we do things around here."

We aim for better. It would be the pinnacle of irony to suggest blowing up playbooks and then offer new "playbooks" in their place. Instead, we want leaders to employ a "first principles" mindset on everything they do. The first principles of business are to figure out what will both delight your customers and be economically viable, and then work to modify the human behavior (of your customers and your people) to make those practices a reality. Most of the time – but not all the time – delighting customers in an economically viable way means adopting new technology because it has the potential to significantly augment the customer experience or significantly lower the cost of delivering the customer experience. If risk needs to be mitigated, we suggest using minimally viable moves. Failure to take timely action isn't mitigating risk; it's just setting your organization up to have fewer degrees of freedom. You'll be left following someone else's best practices, which means average will be your ceiling.

For us, *Detonate* was a mindset book. Could it have been an article (as one of our reviewers suggested)? Maybe. But we did want to provide plenty of evidence of the silly habits businesses have gotten themselves into to give weight to a new way of thinking. Oh, and one last thing we'd like to point out: A lot of people associate "detonate" with chaos and blowing everything up. Actually, that's not what a detonation is; it's a controlled blast that's meant to limit unwanted impact. You blow up what's not working while keeping the thing that is working – a key distinction for businesses that are successful, scaled, and, most important of all, currently profitable.

Provoke is about a single bad habit of business leaders: to wait far too long to act when the future has already revealed itself. We ask our readers to accept a basic premise: Very, very few uncertainties remain uncertain forever. To counteract this habit, we introduce the "if to when" framework for key business trends. We are in the "if" stage if the trend might or might not happen; we are in the "when" phase when the trend will surely happen and it's only a question of timing. Leaders who act in the "if" phase can shape how the trend comes to fruition and provoke the future they want. Leaders who wait are forced to react, including sometimes needing to make the choice to get out of the way (or become a "wind-down business").

Easier said than done, right? Especially because organizations are managed by human beings, who have all sorts of cognitive biases that get in the way of perceiving the shift from "if to when." We offered several mechanisms to help counteract those cognitive biases, including scenario thinking. However, there is no magic formula for knowing whether an "if" trend is becoming a "when" trend. As it turns out, the best defense against cognitive biases is cognitive diversity. Diverse perspectives see different information because lived experiences shape what we notice. Diverse perspectives process that information differently because internal algorithms are based too on those different lived experiences. And diverse perspectives draw different conclusions about the world based on that processing. The more that organizations can take advantage of those different perspectives, the more likely they will have a more comprehensive view of how the world will unfold around them. The stories of our provocateurs – Debbie Bial, Ryan Gravel, and Valerie Rainford – brought these concepts to life. One of the cool opportunities that has come our way since profiling those three is a podcast we now host in collaboration with Thinkers50 in which we invite guests to chat with us about how they have provoked change in the world; it's called *The Provocateurs*.

We hope you know what *Hone* is about given that you've gotten this far. In the context of our broader project, we see *Hone* as a book about rethinking what it means to lead as you steer your organization to and through the future you've provoked, keeping your hands dirty so you don't have to go through the whole cycle of detonation and transformation all over again. The three books together are intended to help established companies reset old operating rules to keep erstwhile successful organizations going for as long a natural life as possible . . . but no longer.

Five Foundational Maxims

As we reflect on our journey, and layer in our learning from our *Hone* artisans, we would like to leave our readers with five foundational maxims that we have discovered in ourselves through the writing process:

A deep understanding of human motivation is key to unlocking secrets. The people we profiled in *Hone* are masters of their crafts because of their attention to other human beings – whether Sam and Onne with their film and photo subjects, Flannery with her guests, or OLP with their audience. Our deep curiosity for what made them tick revealed at least some aspect of each's elemental purpose. Flannery wants to delight with delicious food and an unintrusive atmosphere. Sam wants to capture the story that the subject wants to tell. Onne wants to capture the image in his mind's eye in anticipation of a viewer's reaction. And OLP wants to break down the fourth wall and create a lifelong fan. Business leaders need to be equally curious about the human beings in their orbit, notwithstanding – and perhaps perversely *especially* because of – the rise of AI. We certainly aren't the first and won't be the last to make that assertion. But curiosity about human behavior has to extend well beyond your customers to your employees, your competition, potential collaborators, and the broader community and society. It's through this curiosity that organizations can truly understand the role they can play and influence they can have, which can lead to a virtuous cycle of value creation and positive impact on the world. Conversely, a lack of curiosity will lead to blind spots and dead ends.

To the extent possible, do something where you love the process, not just the outcomes. For someone to become a true master of their craft, they need to be willing to dedicate significant investment to improving over time. There are no shortcuts on the road to mastery. You need to put in the time, and you need to be willing to accept less than perfect performance along the way. Expect to be imperfect at points and be comfortable that occasionally missing the mark is part of the process. The challenge is that if you don't love this process – the necessary hard work and the unavoidable imperfections – you are likely to just stop and never reach a level of mastery. There's a big difference between loving an outcome and loving the process. Athletes love hitting a personal best on a workout, but for every personal best, there are a significant number of slow or weak workouts that are mentally and physically exhausting. It's the same with honing in organizational leadership. Leaders have to know that not every quarter, not every year will go entirely to plan. But loving the process of learning about customers, running new experiments, fine-tuning management systems to make things just a little better, and seeing how your people respond will lead to daily satisfaction.

View action as learning. Unfortunately, too much education is delivered using a classic "professorial" pedagogy – technically known as the "authority teaching style." That is, an expert at the front of the room talking and students taking notes. We know most people learn better by "doing." We see this with young children as their eyes light up in discovery when they conduct their own science experiments, try things out on the playground, or play their first notes on a musical instrument. You can't learn to be an artist without drawing and you can't learn to play an instrument just by listening to lectures on how to do it. Yet, in business, we spend a whole host of time "studying" problems using desk research techniques that mirror the classic professorial approach. What if we created a new orthodoxy where in business, when we aren't sure about something, we conduct a thoughtful and minimally invasive experiment to learn? What if, instead of asking customers what they think, we just placed a few distinctive offers in front of them and saw how they responded? What if, instead of discussing new approaches to meetings with our team, we just tried a few different things and tested how they went?

Walk through life with an eye to how you can improve things. The two of us debated how to phrase this penultimate thought. One of us thought a way to frame it was to consistently be mildly dissatisfied with how everything worked, so that you could try and make it better. The other thought that was perhaps too negative. What we hope to espouse here is that when we look at how things function, we are constantly looking for ways to hone them to make them better. We are both impatient, so we tend to do this every time we have to wait in a line (why are they not using a super-queuing system!?). This pairs with our point above about natural curiosity: If we are too satisfied, we will miss opportunities to make things better. We both see a world that can consistently be improved, in which the status quo is never good enough, and believe that leaders have a responsibility to make it better.

Skilled communication is the lubricant of good leadership. Probably the number-one thing we hear from CEOs whom we work with is that *great* ideas are hard to come by. We agree. There are for sure lots of ideas, but the quality can be, as the kids are saying right now, "sus." In the absence of a slew of great ideas, the most important way to make progress even with "good enough" ideas is to be great at communication. Effective communication inspires, boils an idea down to its core essence, and makes clear the benefits to, and risks of, taking action. Most importantly, clear communication drives the necessary behavior change inside and outside the organization to bring the idea to fruition. When communication isn't clear, it creates *sludge* in the system. We continue to look to business theorist Chris Argyris's ideas for the gold standard of what constitutes great communication: Make your logic clear, ask questions that reveal the logic of others, and above all else, remember, "I have something important to say, but I could be missing something."

HONING THE LIFE JOURNEY

These reflections inform our own approach to life, and our work together has influenced our own mindsets. And all these ideas manifest in our personal lives as well. We both have a long-term goal of health and happiness, and we personally try to hone our approach to life to reach that goal, each with our own foibles and missteps along the way. Both now into our sixth decade, it's become clear that while few generalities can be drawn from individual journeys, one might be that one's relationship with work and consumption doesn't drive happiness. We have also come to learn, since we are both dads, that our most important role – parenting – requires constant honing. There is no "winning" in parenting. You are constantly trying to shape the behavior of another human being, and that takes a lot of learning and tweaking along the way.

With these final reflections, we'll draw things to a close. A devout adherent to old-school vinyl, Geoff is longing to see a box set emerge: all three books bound together with a neat title. *The Reset Trilogy*? *The Sustain Series*? Steve is just shaking his head at how Geoff finds yet another way to reference the music industry in the last bit of the book. Who knows? Maybe on the tenth anniversary of the publication of *Detonate* we'll get something out there. In the meantime, we'll return to where we started with the first words of the first book.

Maybe you love your job.

Maybe you hate it.

Either way, given the collective humanity we are pouring into our jobs, we might as well make them count.

NOTES

CHAPTER 1: THE CHEF

1. *Monitor Deloitte's 2022 Chief Transformation Officer Study – Designing Successful Transformations*, https://www2.deloitte.com/content/dam/Deloitte/us/Documents/consulting/ctro-study-designing-successful-transformations-022822.pdf.
2. Paul A. Argenti, Jenifer Berman, Ryan Calsbeek, and Andrew Whitehouse, "The Secret Behind Successful Corporate Transformations," *Harvard Business Review*, September 14, 2021, https://hbr.org/2021/09/the-secret-behind-successful-corporate-transformations.

CHAPTER 3: THE NERVOUS SYSTEM OF STRATEGY

1. Yves L. Doz, "The Strategic Decisions that Caused Nokia's Failure," INSEAD Knowledge, 2017, https://knowledge.insead.edu/strategy/strategic-decisions-caused-nokias-failure.

CHAPTER 5: WIRING THE NERVOUS SYSTEM

1. Richard M. Ryan and Edward L. Deci, "Self-Determination Theory and the Facilitation of Intrinsic Motivation, Social Development, and Well-Being," *American Psychologist* 55, no. 1 (2000): 68–78, https://selfdeterminationtheory.org/SDT/documents/2000_RyanDeci_SDT.pdf.
2. Christopher F. Schuetze, "Austria Quietly Discards a Vaccine Mandate It Never Enforced," *New York Times*, June 23, 2022, https://www.nytimes.com/2022/06/23/world/europe/austria-covid-vaccine-mandate.html.
3. It's worth noting that while these incentives may have made the office a more attractive destination, they did not necessarily address the underlying reasons for employee reluctance to return. Many companies missed an opportunity to fundamentally reassess the role and purpose of the office in light of the pandemic experience. Rather than merely layering incentives onto the existing office model, a more comprehensive reevaluation of how the physical workspace can best support productivity, collaboration, and

employee well-being might have yielded more sustainable and effective return-to-office strategies.
4. Naomi I. Eisenberger, Matthew D. Lieberman, and Kipling D. Williams, "Does Rejection Hurt? An fMRI Study of Social Exclusion," *Science* 302 (2003): 290–292.
5. Leslie John, Hayley Blunden, and Heidi Liu, "Shooting the Messenger," *Journal of Experimental Psychology: General* 148, no. 4 (April 2019): 644–666.

CHAPTER 6: CHIEF SYSTEM DESIGNER

1. Aaron De Smet, Richard Steele, and Haimeng Zhang, "Shattering the Status Quo: A Conversation with Haier's Heimeng Zhang," *McKinsley Quarterly*, July 27, 2021, https://www.mckinsey.com/capabilities/people-and-organizational-performance/our-insights/shattering-the-status-quo-a-conversation-with-haiers-zhang-ruimin.
2. This concept was explored in depth in Roger Martin's *The Opposable Mind* (2007) and *Creating Great Choices: A Leader's Guide to Integrative Thinking* (2017) (with Jennifer Riel).
3. We devote Chapter 12, "Implications for Leadership: Accelerate by Asking Better Questions," in *Detonate* to this issue.
4. Bryce G. Hoffman, *American Icon: Alan Mulally and the Fight to Save Ford Motor Company* (Crown Currency, 2012).

CHAPTER 7: THE DIRECTOR

1. Nicolas Rapold, "The Filmmaker as Historian: Sam Pollard and 'MLK/FBI,'" *New York Times*, January 15, 2021, https://www.nytimes.com/2021/01/15/movies/sam-pollard-mlk-fbi.html.

CHAPTER 8: PRINCIPLES OF SYSTEM DESIGN

1. NASA Earth Observatory, "World of Change: Aral Sea," https://earthobservatory.nasa.gov/world-of-change/AralSea.
2. Eben Harrell, "A Bold Opening for Chess Player Magnus Carlsen," *TIME*, January 11, 2010, https://time.com/archive/6596910/a-bold-opening-for-chess-player-magnus-carlsen/.
3. Full disclosure: Steve sits on the advisory board of the Smith School of Business at Queen's University in Kingston, Ontario.

4. Association of American Universities, "Lecturers with the Potential for SecurityofEmployment,"https://www.aau.edu/lecturers-potential-security-employment.

Chapter 9: A Recipe for Change

1. Eric Asimov, "Colin Alevras, Inventive New York Chef and Restaurateur, Dies at 51," *New York Times*, October 6, 2022, https://www.nytimes.com/2022/10/06/dining/colin-alevras-dead.html.
2. Frank Bruni, "Stepping Up From Their Starter Homes," *New York Times*, December 6, 2002, https://www.nytimes.com/2006/12/06/dining/reviews/06rest.html.
3. This process is a derivative of the original GrowthPath process created by our friend Bob Lurie and a number of his colleagues (including Geoff!) while at Monitor Group in the 1990s. The original application was to help clients achieve topline revenue growth. Bob and the team had rightly hypothesized that for any company to grow, it has to get people across value chains to behave differently than they do today – customers must pay more for the same thing, customers must buy more of the same product, suppliers must provide better quality material at the same cost, new customers must emerge, etc. After you identify all of those actors, you need to understand all the ways you could motivate these changes. The same principles can be applied to virtually any system comprised of humans when change is the objective.
4. This idea is encapsulated in James Heskett, W. Earl Sasser, and Leonard Schlesinger's service-profit chain model, a popular management framework of the mid-2000s, which isn't used frequently anymore but still holds great wisdom. The model charts the connection between well-managed employees and profitability. Specifically, it posits that profit and growth are primarily stimulated by customer loyalty, which is a direct result of customer satisfaction. Satisfaction, in turn, is largely influenced by the value of services provided to customers, and this value is created by satisfied, loyal, and productive employees. Employee satisfaction, therefore, is a critical factor, and it results primarily from high-quality support services and policies that enable employees to deliver results to customers.

Chapter 10: Walking the Talk

1. Parts of our business are subject to various regulations, and we always comply as required.

2. We do this distinctly based on whether we are the auditor of our client.
3. Similarly, this construct is applied distinctly based on whether we are the auditor of a client.

CHAPTER 13: MINIMALLY VIABLE THOUGHTS: HONING OUR FUTURE

1. Steven Goldbach, Geoff Tuff, and Derek Pankratz, "Don't Bet Against the Move to Clean Energy," *MIT Sloan Management Review*, September 17, 2024, https://sloanreview.mit.edu/article/dont-bet-against-the-move-to-clean-energy/.
2. Claire Dougherty, Charlotte Emerson, Laura Hutchinson, Maeve Masterson, and Chandler Randol, "Clean Energy 101: Demand Aggregation," *RMI*, September 18, 2024, https://rmi.org/demand-aggregation-101/.

Acknowledgments

This book would not have made it to our publisher without the tireless and multifaceted work of Megan Buskey – or at least not on time and in a coherent format. Our editor, Eben Harrell, also worked relentlessly to improve the product and make two guys who think very similarly but communicate starkly differently sound like roughly one voice. Immense thanks to both of you in particular.

Sue Nersessian lived the entire journey with us, providing terrific input and keeping us from doing anything stupid. Meghan Stark, Anita Soucy, Julia Talvas, Krissy Loughran, Kristine Orbrecht, Marc Cohen, and John Treiber also kept us out of stupid territory – thank you for your careful reviews. Derek Pankratz led our research team, which included Mildreth Campos, Rafael Delatorre, Shefi Gupta, Maria Downing, and Julius Tapper. We were lucky that Kat Jiwani agreed to reprise her role as "Copyedit Queen," with Mildreth also providing copyediting support.

Terra Sorensen helped manage the whole operation, especially as we got the project off the ground. Colleen LeMay and Grace Guttierez made sure that Geoff and Steve, respectively, had time and headspace to put toward writing, even as the urgency of day-to-day responsibilities remained unabated. Thank you all for making sure this adventure did not wander off track.

Tom Fishburne has once again saved our readers thousands of words with his illustrations – and likely provided them some well-earned breathing room in the midst of all the remaining words – and we thank him and his wife and business partner, Tallie, for agreeing to go for a third ride with us.

We have been so blessed to have many colleagues, friends, and family who have been willing to engage with our ideas and challenge us to make them better. Among those who were willing to read and push us to hone our work further were Dan Helfrich, Pete Shimer, Ben Campbell, Des Dearlove, Stuart Crainer (who deserves an additional thank-you for telling us not to call the book "Tinker"), Paul Polman, Jonathan Goodman, Michelle Dunstan, Rider Tuff, and Kwasi Mitchell. Collectively, thank you! Eliza Wright is to be credited for spontaneously inventing the term "ornamental purpose" as she wandered through the Tuff living room during one of Steve and Geoff's working sessions – thanks, Eliza! Thank you also to Brian Quinn, George Fackler, and Roger Martin for your ideation early on. A big thank you to Jason Girzadas, Joe Ucuzoglu, and Lara Abrash for your input and all your support.

We don't have a time machine and, as of this writing, we are not sure who will be helping us from Deloitte's marketing and PR team. But based on our previous experiences, we know that you will be fantastic; please consider yourself sincerely thanked by us.

We would also like to acknowledge the role that AI played in writing this book. As a couple of authors in the innovation space, it would be inconsistent with our desired brand positioning not to try out the new tools available in the world. Did AI write this book? No. It's not ready to do that and based on our experiences thus far, it's not something we'd want to use for that purpose. True creativity and framing up something new or presented in a fresh way is harder for AI, which is, naturally, based on everything that has come previously. AI was really helpful to us in thinking up lots of examples to consider (which used to take our research team lots of time). It also was helpful for editing suggestions. Finally, it proved humorous from time to time with some hallucinations. We can imagine a world where AI is an important writing tool in the future, and people should leverage it to make their work better.

The artisans we feature throughout deserve thanks for their willingness to open up to us about their lives and livelihoods, and for being a source of inspiration and learning as the ideas came together. There's no doubt that the ideas improved as we worked through analogies to the worlds of Flannery Klette-Kolton, Onne van der Wal, Sam Pollard, and Raine Maida and Duncan Coutts from the band Our Lady Peace.

Finally, thank you to our families:

From Geoff: Thanks, Mart, for episodically and straightforwardly reminding me that I can be "a lot" . . . and most of the time doing it with a smile. I'm sure that pacing and thinking around a New York City apartment did nothing to convince you that your husband is entering his mellower years. Rider, Quinn, Mason, and Hunter: Thanks for continuing to grow and demonstrate that very cool and impressive things can be accomplished in the world without decades of experience if you have a sense of adventure and willingness to just try.

From Steve: Thank you, Michelle, for supporting this "hobby" of mine and reading the book and telling us, "It's a book." Grayson, thank you for telling Daddy to get to work, even though you know that I know that you really just wanted to control the TV and watch some *MasterChef*. Both of you, thank you for all the brainstorming that went into the title and humoring me when I wanted to talk about the book at family dinner. Mom and Dad, thanks for instilling in me a lifelong desire to learn, and Dad, special thanks for emailing Geoff after every podcast he hosts.

About the Authors

Geoff Tuff is a principal at Deloitte Consulting LLP, where he has held various positions across the firm's Sustainability, Innovation, and Strategy practices. At the time of this writing, he leads all sustainability work globally and in the US for clients in the energy, resources, and industrials sectors. In the past, he led the innovation firm Doblin and was a senior partner at Monitor Group, serving as a member of its global board of directors before the company was acquired by Deloitte. He has been with some form of Monitor for over 30 years.

Geoff's work centers on helping clients transform their businesses to grow and compete in nontraditional ways. Over the course of his career, Geoff has worked in virtually every industry, and he uses that breadth of experience to bring novel insights about how things might operate to clients stuck in industry conventional wisdom. He is valued for his integrative approach to solving problems and combines deep analytic and strategic expertise with a natural orientation toward approaches embodied in design thinking.

Geoff is a frequent speaker and writer on the topic of growth through innovation and has written for a variety of outlets, including *Harvard Business Review*. He holds degrees from Dartmouth College and Harvard Business School.

Steven Goldbach believes that strategy, at its core, is about shaping a better future. After spending nearly a decade as Deloitte's chief strategy officer, Steve now leads Deloitte's Sustainability practice in the US, channeling his passion for impactful change into building a world in which businesses see sustainability as an opportunity, not an obligation.

Prior to joining Deloitte, Steve held numerous leadership positions at Monitor and served as head of strategy at Forbes Magazine

Group. Steve sits on the advisory boards of the Smith School of Business at Queen's University, Kingston, Ontario, and the New York Botanical Garden. He holds degrees from Queen's University and Columbia Business School.

Geoff and Steve's first book, *Detonate: Why – and How – Corporations Must Blow Up Best Practices (and Bring a Beginner's Mind) to Survive*, was released under the Wiley imprint in 2018. Their follow-up book, *Provoke: How Leaders Shape the Future by Overcoming Fatal Human Flaws*, arrived in 2021. Each book has been featured on a variety of national bestseller lists, including the *Wall Street Journal*'s. Both led to Geoff and Steve's short-listing for Thinkers50's Distinguished Achievement Award in Strategy in 2019 and the same in Leadership in 2021. They are co-hosts of the monthly podcast *Provocateurs: Profiles in Leadership*.

INDEX

A

Accessibility ERGs, 126
Accessibility improvements, 127
Accountability, of CEOs, 120
Accountability director, 46
Active listening, 7, 44–45, 167–168
Adaptation, 148–149, 173
Advocacy, for policy changes, 102
Agility, xiv, 137, 173–175
Allyship, 127
American work culture, 153–157
Anecdotes, 141
Assumptions, challenging, 151
Autonomy, 72

B

Baby Boomers, 109–110
Balance:
    of employee care and business demands, 68–69
    of expectations from all sides, 36–37
    of high-level goals and daily realities, 142–143
    as role of leadership, 144–145
    strategic thinking with day-to-day management, 30–31
Behaviors, embracing new, 7–8
Belarusian work culture, 153–155
Belonging, 128
Biases, 12, 27
Bigger picture, seeing, 18–19, 75–76
Bottlenecks, ix–x
BRIDGE formula, 13–14, 55–58
Budget (BRIDGE formula), 55
Build Relationships (BRIDGE formula), 13
Burnout, 166–167
Business demands, 68–69
Business plan approach, 55–58
Business structures, changing, 162–163

C

CEOs, *see* Chief executive officers
CFOs (chief financial officers), 122
Change, resilience and, 174
Checkbox mentality, 84–86
"Check the box" management, 18–19, 98–100
Chief executive officers (CEOs), 117–133
    accountability of, 120
    as balancing act, 144–145
    balancing high-level goals with daily realities, 142–143
    calendars and values of, 138–140
    challenges facing, 117–119

Chief executive officers
(CEOs) *(Continued)*
creating a culture of listening,
140–141
humanizing leadership, 141–142
maintaining composure, 121–123
risk of "yes people," 123–124
as unique roles, 131–132
visionary leadership
of, 124–131
Chief financial officers
(CFOs), 122
Chief human resource officers
(CHROs), 122
Chiefs of staff, 122
Collaboration:
cross-functional, 171
with different generations, 109–111
with organizational
influencers, 13
as role of managers, ix–x
through technology, 129–130
with your team, 41
Collective success, 6–7
Communication:
about business impact of
teams, 85–86
across cultures, 153–157
balancing expectations
with, 41–42
and engagement, 100
HR aiding, 113
by leaders, 130–131
between leadership and
teams, 59–60

open and transparent, 72
strategic, 43–45
Company values, 55, 98
Compassionate productivity,
79–88
beyond the checkbox
mentality, 84–86
and continuous
learning, 86–87
fairness and flexibility in,
81–83
and hiring process, 83
Compensation, 92, 163–165
Compliance policies, 91
Composure, maintaining,
121–123
Conflict resolution, 92
Connection(s), 135–146
balancing high-level goals and
daily realities, 142–143
calendars reflecting values,
138–140
CEOs fostering, 124–131
creating a culture of
listening, 140–141
fostering, with vulnerability
and relatability, 144
humanizing leadership,
141–142
between leadership and
teams, 59–60
leadership as balancing
act, 144–145
managing by walking
around, 136–138
with organizational
influencers, 13–14
with team members, 9–10

Constructive feedback, 67, 111–112, 115, 170
Continuous learning:
   and compassionate productivity, 86–87
   for experienced managers, 114–115
   for modern leaders, 148–149
   valuing, 22
Core teams, 121–123
COVID-19 pandemic, 71
Crises, 70–72, 118
Cross-cultural training, 155, 157
Cross-functional alignment, x
Cross-functional collaboration, 171
Culture(s):
   of accountability and engagement, 98
   acknowledging employees', 166
   of continuous improvement, 31
   creating, as manager, 68
   and global workforce, 153–155
   of listening, 140–141
   at Microsoft, 129–130
   of openness, 28
   of proactive problem-solving, x
   of psychological safety, 72–73
   of shared ownership, x
Culture of excellence, 164–178
   agility in, 173–175
   CEO's role in, 136, 144
   core teams in, 121
   creating, xiii–xiv, 152–153
   driving collective success, 6
   driving continuous improvement of, 176–178
   fostering connections in, 124, 128
   respect in, 164–169
   solution-oriented thinking in, 170–172
Curiosity, 74, 111

D

Data security policies, 91
Day-to-day management, 30–31, 36
Decision-making, 165–166, 173
Define Goals (BRIDGE formula), 13
Delegate (DIGS formula), 66–67
Delegation, 30–31
Deloitte, 109
Demographics, 164
Development (BRIDGE Formula), 57
Diamonds, recognizing, 64–66
DIGS formula, 66–67
Discomfort, 151–152
Disruption, 108
Diversity:
   benefits of, 99
   as catalyst for innovation, 84
   in personal board of directors, 47
   of workforce, 164

E

Education, formal, 151
Emerging leaders, 17–33
   balancing strategic thinking with day-to-day management, 30–31

Emerging leaders *(Continued)*
   changing responsibilities of, 18–19
   establishing a strategic foundation, 31–32
   risk management and productivity, 19–25
   talent development and succession planning, 25–29
Emotional intelligence (EQ), 149–150
Empathy, 129
Employees:
   acknowledging cultures and religions of, 166
   actively listening to, 167–168
   balancing business demands and well-being of, 68–69
   in crisis, 70
   daily realities of, 143
   empowering, 152–153, 170
   managing well-being of, 41–42
   personal boundaries of, 166–167
   remaining connected with, 124–131
Employee feedback policies, 92
Employee resource groups (ERGs), 126–128
Empower (REE method), 72
Empowerment, 152–153, 170
Engagement, 99
Enron, 118
EQ (emotional intelligence), 149–150
ERGs (employee resource groups), 126–128
Ernst & Young, 142
Ethics policies, 91
Evaluate and Adjust (BRIDGE formula), 14
Evaluation (BRIDGE Formula), 58
Expectations, balancing, 36–37
Experienced managers, 107–116
Experiential learning, 150
Express (REE method), 72

F
Fairness, 28, 81–83, 102
Feedback:
   in culture of listening, 140–141
   encouraging, 124, 170
   and engagement, 100
   giving constructive, 67
   honest and constructive, 111–112, 115
Feedback loops, 45
Firm-wide policies, 101–103
First-time managers, 1–16
   building trust, 4–5
   connecting with organizational influencers, 13–14
   establishing team values and a social contract, 12
   good habits for, 14–15
   laying a solid foundation for, 10–11
   navigating inherited peer dynamics, 8–10
   new behaviors for, 7–8
   as outside hires, 3–4
   pitfalls for, 11–12

rookie mistakes of, 5–7
transitioning from team member to, 2–3
Flattening organizations, 162–163
Flexibility, 81–83, 143, 173
Formal education, 151

G

Generate Solutions (BRIDGE formula), 14
Generations, 109–111, 164
Generation X, 110
Generation Z, 110
Give (DIGS formula), 67
Globalization, 148–149
Global workforce, 153–157
Goals:
    balancing high-level goals and daily realities, 142–143
    balancing short- and long-term, 39
    setting clear, 13
Growth:
    opportunities for, 167
    personal, 151–152
    support for continuous, 67
    of team members, 22
Growth (BRIDGE Formula), 57
Growth mindset, 129, 173

H

Harvard Business Review, 100
Heads of communications, 122
Health and safety policies, 90–91
Hiring process, 83, 163
HR (human resources), 112–113, 115
HR Business Partners (HRBPs), 112–113
HR policies, 103
Huffington, Arianna, 142
Human resources (HR), 112–113, 115
Hurricane Sandy, 70
Hybrid workplaces, 139

I

ICs (individual contributors), 2–3
Impact (BRIDGE formula), 56–57
Inclusion, in decision-making, 165–166
Inclusive projects, 127
Indian work culture, 155–157
Individual contributors (ICs), 2–3
Influencers, organizational, 13–14
Inherited peer dynamics, 8–10
Initiate Collaboration (BRIDGE formula), 13
Initiative, rewarding, 170–171
Innovation, 76
Inspiration, 152
Instructional learning, 151
International workforce, 138–139, 153–157
Introspection, 11–12
Invest (DIGS formula), 67
Isolation, 48–49

K

Key performance indicators (KPIs), 20–21
Knowledge, of policies, 101–102

L

Leadership, 147–159
  as balancing act, 144–145
  building emotional intelligence, 149–150
  compassionate, 80
  connecting teams and, 59–60
  continuous learning and adaptation in, 148–149
  creating a culture of excellence, 152–153
  critical skills for, 148
  cultivating, 77
  as daily choice, 178–179
  demonstrating potential for, 74
  by example, 130
  of experienced managers, 107–116
  facing challenges in, xii
  future of, 162–164
  humanizing, 141–142
  as journey, 15
  as a journey, xv
  managing crises, 119
  navigating a global workforce, 153–157
  people as focus of, 179
  policy, 103
  with precision and purpose, 60
  purpose of, x
  role of, at highest levels, 131–132
  stages of, xv
  thriving as, 158
  types of learning for, 150–152
  understanding expectations of, 44
  visionary, 54, 113–114, 124–131
Learning:
  continuous, *see* Continuous learning
  mistakes as opportunities for, 22
  types of, 150–152
LGBTQ+ ERGs, 127
LinkedIn, 142
Listening, 7, 44–45, 140–141, 167–168
Listening tours, 129
Loneliness, 48–49
Long-term goals, 39

M

McKinsey, 99
Manager allyship training, 127
Managers, ix–x. *See also specific types of*
Managing by walking around, 136–138, 144
Marketplace policies, 97–98
Microsoft, 129–130
Middle managers, 35–51
  balancing expectations from all sides, 36–37
  challenges faced by, 37–39
  importance of, 49–50
  loneliness of, 48–49
  managing employee well-being, 41–42
  personal board of directors for, 42–43, 45–48

prioritization, 39–41
as strategic communicators, 43–45
Millennials, 110
Mistakes, 5–7, 22
Multicultural networks, 127

N
Nadella, Satya, 129–130
Network, creating, 13, 31

O
Objectives and key results (OKRs), 20–22
Observation(s), 4, 67
Onboarding, 94–95
One-on-one meetings, 7, 9–10, 26–27
Open office hours, 139
Open roles, on public platforms, 85
Organizational influencers, 13–14
Organizational insights director, 46
Outside hires, as managers, 3–4

P
Peer dynamics, 8–11, 36–37
Performance management:
  "check the box" mentality toward, 100
  driving continuous improvement with, 176–178
  metrics for, 20–22
  Team Agility and High-Performance Monitoring Chart, 174–175
  Team Respect and High-Performance Monitoring Chart, 168–169
  Team Solution-Oriented Thinking and High-Performance Monitoring Chart, 171–172
Personal anecdotes, 141
Personal board of directors, 42–43, 45–48
Personal boundaries, 166–167
Personal values, 8
Physical environment, 95–97
Policies, 89–105
  and "check the box" management, 98–100
  highlighting benefits of, 84–85
  HR, 103
  impact of policy leadership, 103
  influencing marketplace, 97–98
  influencing workforce, 93–95
  influencing workplace, 95–97
  managing firm-wide, 101–103
  translating policies into actions, 90–92
Policy leadership, 103
Potential:
  biases limiting, 27
  identify and nurture, 57
  long-term view on, 76–77
  recognizing, 64–66
  redefining, 73–76
Precision, leading with, 60
Preconceptions, 108–111
Prioritization, 39–41, 142–143
Proactive problem-solving, x

Problem-solving. *See also* Solution-oriented thinking
culture of proactive, x
empowering employees for, 170
increasing, with changing business structures, 163
Productivity:
and belonging, 128
compassionate, *see* Compassionate productivity
and risk management, 19–25
Promotions, 95
Psychological safety, 71–73
Public platforms, open roles on, 85
Purpose, 60, 114–115

Q
Quota fatigue, 84

R
Recognition:
for initiative, 170–171
of personal board of directors, 48–49
as respect, 167
of team members, 72
Recognize (REE method), 72
REE method, 72–73
Reflective learning, 151
Relatability, 144
Relationships. *See also* Connection(s)
with HR, 112–113, 115
with organizational influencers, 13
with personal board of directors, 47–48
Religion, 166
Remote workplaces, 139
Remote work policies, 92, 96
Research Needs (BRIDGE formula), 13
Resilience, 76, 174
Resource director, 46–47
Resources (BRIDGE formula), 56
Respect, xiii, 5, 137, 164–169
Retention, 22, 94–95, 163
Risk:
management of, 19–25
of potential, 65
of "yes people," 123–124
Risk matrices, 23–25

S
Safety, psychological, 71–73
Scope, widening your, 31
Scrutiny, of CEOs, 121–123
Self-examination, 151
Senior managers, 53–61
BRIDGE formula, 55–58
connecting leadership and teams, 59–60
crafting strategic plans, 54
leading with precision and purpose, 60
multiple functions managed by, 58–59
Short-term goals, 39
Social contracts, 12
Social learning, 150–151

Solutions, generating, 14
Solution-oriented thinking, xiv, 137, 170–172
Sponsorship programs, 127
Standardization, of policies, 102
Status quo, challenging, 108–111
Strategic communicators, 43–45
Strategic plans, 54
Strategic thinking, 30–31, 36, 69
Succession planning, 25–29, 92
Support:
   of CEOs, 119–120
   of employees, 70–72
   of personal board of directors, 48–49
   providing to your team, 41
Support (DIGS formula), 67
Sustainable practices, 97–98

T

Talent, attracting, 22–23, 93–94, 163
Talent Architects, 63–78
   balancing employee care and business demands, 68–69
   creating a culture of psychological safety, 72–73
   DIGS formula, 66–67
   long-term view on potential, 76–77
   recognizing potential, 64–66
   redefining potential, 73–76
   supporting employees, 70–72
Talent development, 25–29. *See also* Talent Architects
   capacity for, 73
   identify and nurture potential, 57
   policies on, 92
Teams:
   as assets, 69
   collective success of, 6–7
   communicate business impact of, 85–86
   connecting leadership and, 59–60
   creating and developing, xi–xii
   evaluating resources for, 56
   managing well-being of, 38–39
   measuring agility of, 174–175
   measuring respect of, 168–169
   measuring solution-oriented thinking of, 171–172
   performance scores of, 176–178
   as priority of new managers, 10–11
   setting new precedents with, 6
   tailoring policies to fit needs of, 102
   unique values of individual members, 8
Team Agility and High-Performance Monitoring Chart, 174–175
Team High-Performance Scores, 176–178
Team Respect and High-Performance Monitoring Chart, 168–169
Team Solution-Oriented Thinking and High-Performance Monitoring Chart, 171–172

Team values, 12
Technology:
   collaboration through, 129–130
   and continuous learning, 148
   to track team members' development and contributions, 29
Tesla, 118
Thriving, 50, 147–159, 173
Transparency:
   about promotions, 95
   in communication, 40, 72, 130
   in compensation, 165
   and culture of listening, 140–141
   as key behavior, 7–8
   by middle managers, 38
Trust, 4–5, 83

U
Uber, 118
UK work culture, 155–157
Unlearning, 149, 151

V
Values:
   calendars reflecting, 138–140
   of the company, 55, 98
   of individual team members, 8
Virtual environment, 95–97
Visionary leadership, 54, 113–114, 124–131
Vulnerability, 144

W
Walking the floors, 136–138, 144
Walmart, 118
Women in ERGs, 126
Workforce:
   diversity in, 164
   global, 153–157
   policies concerning, 93–95
Workplaces:
   creating excellent, 153
   policies concerning, 95–97

Y
"Yes people," 123–124